DOGS

WHAT DOG FOR ME?

Robert V. Masters

GALAHAD BOOKS • NEW YORK CITY

1966 Printing

Sterling Book of Dogs © 1962

What Dog for Me?

All rights reserved

Published by Galahad Books, New York, N.Y.

This book reprinted with permission of Sterling

Publishing Co., Inc., New York, N.Y.

Library of Congress Catalog Card Number: 73-76739

ISBN: 0-88365-014-2

Printed in the United States of America

Contents

INTRODUCTION

As this book will show you, there are many breeds of dogs and they all have different appeals. The emphasis in this book is on pets and not on show dogs, field dogs or hunting dogs, although they are included. An important consideration in choosing a dog—even more important than its appearance, its size or its temperament—is its availability. Not all breeds of dogs are available in every locality. You will find some breeds omitted in this book because they are not easily obtained in the United States or Great Britain. For example, the Mexican Hairless is a fine little pet but extremely rare. The Bernese Mountain Dog is rare also.

Some breeds that have not been recognized as yet by the American Kennel Club or its British counterpart have, however, been included because they are available: two Australian dogs, the Silky Terrier and the Australian Terrier; the Akita from Japan; and the English Shepherd dog.

The dogs are arranged in alphabetical order rather than in A.K.C. categories. The most usual way of talking about a dog has been the determining factor for its alphabetical listing. If you do not find a breed where you think it should be, use the index which has all cross references.

The photographs shown picture the best-looking dogs according to A.K.C. standards. These pictures have come from the foremost breeders and kennels in the nation. Dogs like those in the pictures can become your pets.

STANDARDS AS DETERMINED BY AMERICAN KENNEL CLUB
HEADS

BROKEN UP FACE, LAY BACK

BUMPY SKULL

CHEEKY

DOMED HEAD

DOWN FACE

DISH FACE

FROG FACE

SNIPEY MUZZLE

TAILS

CRANK TAIL

GAY TAIL

OTTER TAIL

RING TAIL

PLUME

SABER TAIL

SCREW TAIL

SICKLE TAIL

SQUIRREL TAIL

10

EARS

BAT EAR

BUTTON EAR

DROP EAR

PRICK EAR

ROSE EAR

SEMI-PRICK EAR

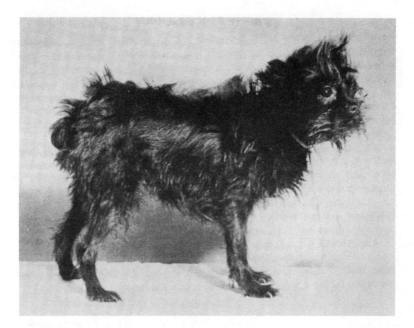

Ch. Alfa von Elmuer has had four Best of Breeds in six shows. His muzzle is unusually short. This Affenpinscher is owned by Elmuer Kennels of Rensselaer, New York.

AFFENPINSCHER

Size: Shoulder height not exceeding 10¼". *Weight:* 7 to 8 pounds. *Standard:* Small but rather sturdy in build and not delicate. Carries himself with comical seriousness. Generally quiet but can get vehemently excited. Coat short and dense in certain parts, shaggy and long in others, but should be hard and wiry; loose and shaggy on legs and around eyes, nose and chin, giving typical monkey-like appearance. Colors: black with tan markings, red, gray and other mixtures.

The Affenpinscher or "Monkey Dog" (so named for his monkeyish expression) is a game, alert, intelligent and sturdy breed, progenitor of the more familiar Brussels Griffon. His ragged expression comes from his bushy eyebrows, chin with hair tuft and moustache. Characteristic of the breed is a protruding chin and dark flashing eyes showing his terrier spirit. Although he is toy in size, he is far from frail. Never destructive, the Affenpinscher can be lovable and full of fun. He is gaining in popularity in the United States.

One peculiar characteristic of the breed is that he sheds his coat partially once a year. After about two weeks of combing, the period ends. The wiry hairs do not cling to materials or furniture, making him an ideal house dog.

13

AFGHAN HOUND

Size: Male, 26″ to 28″ high; female, 24″ to 26″ high. *Weight:* Male, about 60 pounds; female, about 50 pounds. *Standard:* Straight front, long, proudly carried head, prominent nasal bone structure, eyes gazing into distance. Strikingly long, silky topknot. Peculiar coat pattern. Very prominent hip bones, large feet, profuse trouserings. Ears long, covered with long, silky hair. Eyes almond-shaped. Neck long, strong and arched. Body back line practically level from shoulders to loin. Tail with ring or curve on end. Colors: all colors and combinations.

One of the most ancient breeds, the Afghan has been called the Dog of Noah's Ark by tribesmen hunters in Afghanistan. The Afghan or a long-haired dog of this greyhound type was pictured in Egypt in 4000 B.C. Afghans were hunters working in pairs against antelopes, gazelles and even the dangerous snow leopards. The first Afghans known to the West came to England in the 1890's but did not become popular until the 1920's. Shortly afterward this aristocratic breed arrived for the first time in America.

The Afghan is suitable for both country and city life, being content to lead a quiet life with a daily constitutional in the city streets. He is well-mannered, gentle, seldom barks, is highly intelligent and readily trained. Though reserved with strangers, the Afghan is a great clown with the family.

Ch. Shirkhan of Grandeur has won many Best in Shows including the Westminster. This Afghan is owned by Sunny Shay of Grandeur Kennels, Hicksville, Long Island, N. Y.

No wonder this champion Airedale looks proud, surrounded by all his ribbons and trophies. Yet an Airedale need not be a prize winner to be a good pet.

AIREDALE TERRIER

Size: 22" to 23" high. *Weight:* 40 to 50 pounds. *Standard:* Upstanding, squarely built. Long head, powerful jaw. Eyes dark and small, lips tight. Shoulders long and sloping well into back, body short, back level. Root of tail well up on back, carried gaily, not curved but docked. Coat hard, dense and wiry, lying straight and close. Movement free in action. Colors: head and ears tan, body tan or black or dark grizzle with red mixture often found.

The Airedale originated about 100 years ago in the Aire River Valley in England. He is thought to be a cross between the Old English Terrier and the Otter Hound. A dog that becomes faithfully attached to his owners, he makes a fine companion and great protector. The Airedale, still used for hunting large game in Africa, India and Canada, was also among the first breeds chosen for police duty in Germany and Great Britain. He is a dependable dispatch carrier because of his ability to suffer wounds without faltering and has been used in several wars. His sweet disposition particularly endears him to women. When mature, he has a dignified aloofness with strangers and other dogs.

AKITA

Size: Male, 25½" to 27½" high; female, 22½" to 24½" high. *Weight:* In proportion to height and length. *Standard:* Massive, muscular, with well-knit frame; male compact, female rangy and somewhat wolf-like. Massive, broad head, flat at top of skull, stop well marked but not abrupt; free from wrinkles, cheeks full but not loose. Muzzle moderate length, squarish jaws, large black wide nose. Fairly small prick-ears wide at base, carried erect and slightly forward over eyes. Medium eyes as dark as possible. Strong muscular legs, forelegs having 10° to 15° angle of pastern to foot, hind legs moving together at full run to permit ready spring when hunting. Tail conspicuously large, set high, curled over back. Double coat, medium-long, stiff and harsh; undercoat thick and furry. Colors: fawn, red, dim-brindle (cat-striped), all grays and silvers, white markings.

The Akita is the large size of the ancient Japanese pure breed, Nippon Inu, which dates back 5000 years according to archaeological finds in shell burial mounds. People of the New Stone Age, still unacquainted with agriculture, kept dogs to assist them in hunting. The Akita today is a courageous, good-natured dog, extremely affectionate and sensitive to kindness by his master. He is an intrepid hunter of deer, bear and wild boar, but adapts easily to suburban or city life.

Left: Silver Crown Princess poses for her master, Maurice L. Simmons, who with Kenneth M. Nichols owns the Silver Crown Akita Kennels in Winona, Washington. Below: The Akita appears on a 2-yen stamp of Japan.

The Duke of Valdez, an all white Alaskan Eskimo owned by Mrs. Mae M. Carpenter of Redwood City, California.

ALASKAN ESKIMO (Malamute)

Size: Male, 22″ to 25″ high; female, 2″ less. *Weight:* Male, 65 to 85 pounds; female, 50 to 70 pounds. *Standard:* Well-proportioned head, broad and wedge-shaped with a strong flat skull and powerful jaws. Nose large and brown or black in color. Lips same color, medium-length muzzle. Eyes small but deep-set, short ears erect and turned forward. Neck short and muscular. Forequarters broad, big-boned and muscular, as are hindquarters, which are medium length with the stifles well bent. Large bushy tail carried curled up over the back or held aloft. Paws large with fur between very thick pads. Coat extremely dense with long guard hairs and wool undercoat. All known colors and all combinations, but all white or white with black head most common.

The Alaskan Eskimo (named after the Malamute tribe) is a working dog of such courage and physical endurance that he is indispensable to men living in the Arctic regions. He gives an impression of rugged sturdiness. His dense coat makes him impervious to weather down to 70° below zero, but he is unhappy in temperatures of over 70° above. When raised as a pet, he is a wonderful family dog, fond of children and a good watchdog. He is very quiet with no bark at all and seldom utters the yelps or howls of which he is capable in the wilds of the far north. He is very healthy, with a quick intelligence and retentive memory.

The Alaskan Eskimo is far more affectionate with humans than with other dogs or animals. Because he is sometimes inclined to be pugnacious when other animals are around, it may be a good idea to restrict his liberty.

AMERICAN WATER SPANIEL

Size: 15″ to 18″ high. *Weight:* 25 to 45 pounds. *Standard:* Sturdily built, not too compact, legs of medium length. Broad, full skull with deep muzzle and wide-set eyes. Long ears covered with curls, falling close. Coat thick and closely curled, feathered tail hanging rocker-like. Colors: solid liver or dark chocolate.

A true native American developed within the last 50 years, this Spaniel is the equal of any hunting dog. He will lead you unbelievably close to pheasants, grouse, quail, etc., flush them and then retrieve them. Neither zero weather nor icy water will keep him from swimming out to retrieve ducks and geese. This natural-born hunter of waterfowl and upland birds learns to hunt in just a few hours! He is the easiest of all dogs to housebreak, too, and is very fond of children.

These curly American Water Spaniels love to swim, summer or winter, and range the wide acres of Paul L. Bovee's Bovee Farm Kennels, Plainfield, Wisconsin.

AUSTRALIAN TERRIER

Size: About 10″ high. *Weight:* Between 9 and 14 pounds. *Standard:* (Not recognized by A.K.C.) Head long, skull flat, long powerful terrier jaws. Eyes are small, dark and bright. Ears small, set high and pricked. Body rather long and proportioned to height. Longish neck. Tail docked, leaving a generous ⅔. Outstanding characteristic is neck ruff and soft head topknot compared to harsher, weather-resistant, 2½″ long coat. Feet and muzzle smooth-coated. Nose dark. Colors: blue-black, silvery impression with rich tan on legs and face; or whole coat bright clear red or sandy.

Originally known as the Broken-Coated Terrier and the Australian Rough

The male, Willelva Wanderer, is the darker blue and tan dog in the picture. He was the first Aussie to win an obedience degree. He was imported from famous Australian kennels by Pleasant Pasture Kennels. The female is blue and tan and is also imported. Her name is Elvyne Blue Taffeta. Both are owned by Nell N. Fox of Pleasant Pasture Kennels, Point Pleasant, New Jersey.

Terrier, this dog has been bred from Skye, Black-and-Tan, Scottish Dandie Dinmont with a small percentage of Irish and Yorkshire terriers. The breed made its debut in 1957 at the Westminster Kennel Show in New York. Although not recognized in the United States, the breed is recognized in every other English-speaking country.

An ideal house dog, he is rugged enough for outdoors. Excellent as a watch-dog and with children, the little Aussie had his guard instinct developed through being used for alarms around the old gold mines. He is not yappy, nervously excitable or aggressive with other dogs. Long-lived, deeply loyal and affection-ate, the Australian Terrier is hardy, and adaptable to any condition or climate.

The Aussie makes a good pet because he is toy in size, requires little trim-ming, is clean in all ways, easy to train and economical to feed. His fine ability as a rodent and snake killer no doubt adds to his popularity in India.

BASENJI

Size: 16" to 17" high. *Weight:* 22 to 25 pounds. *Standard:* Small, lightly built, with short level back, deep chest, strong muscular hindquarters, hocks well down, well-sprung ribs and deep brisket ending in a definite waist. Appears high on the leg compared to its length as legs are straight with clean fine bone and long forearm. Flat, well-chiseled skull of medium width, with foreface tapering from eye to muzzle and shorter than skull. Fine and profuse wrinkles on forehead and on side. Rounded muzzle ends with jet black nose. Dark hazel eyes are almond-shaped, obliquely set and far-seeing as well as alert. Small pointed ears set well forward on top of head stand erect. Short and silky coat over unusually pliant skin. Tail curls tightly over to either side. Colors: chestnut red (the deeper the better) or pure black, or black and tan, all with white feet, chest and tail tip.

Known as the "barkless dog" (he is naturally barkless), the Basenji breed is as old as the Nile, having been the pet of Pharaohs of ancient Egypt. Yet he is new to America and England. He followed mankind in his migrations throughout the world, although his native land is Central Africa where he is highly prized for his intelligence, speed, hunting skill and for his silence. It was only in 1937 that he became generally known to England and America, but similar breeds have been traced in northern Europe, Asia, the South Seas, Ceylon and the Malayan states.

Built like a Fox Terrier, the Basenji is often compared to a deer for his beauty, graceful and poised carriage, and keen intelligence. One outstanding feature is his coat, silky fine and shining like burnished copper in the sun to which he is quite accustomed. His hunting prowess is well demonstrated by native Africans who use him for pointing (he can scent at 80 yards!), retrieving, driving game into nets and hunting wounded quarry. His silence is a great asset. Apartment dwellers also appreciate this extraordinary aspect of the Basenji who makes a

BASENJI
Ch. Rhosenji's Adok stands at attention for his owner and breeder, George L. Gilkey of Rhosenji Kennels, Merrill, Wisconsin.

distinctive sound, a cross between a yodel and chortle, only when he is particularly happy and only for those he loves. (He will cry when left alone, like all puppies, but this passes as soon as he's reassured of his family's return.) Yet, he makes a superb watchdog, even without a bark, and an intruder would have a bad time trying to get past him.

Another asset is his fastidiousness—he cleans himself all over like a cat, and under ordinary conditions a Basenji never needs a bath! An occasional brushing is all he requires. One endearing mannerism he has is teasing someone to play by bringing one front paw behind his ear, down over his nose and repeating this until he attracts attention. But when play is over, the Basenji relaxes peacefully and is content to lie right at his master's feet.

BASSET HOUND

Size: Shoulder height 11" to 15" high. *Weight:* 25 to 45 pounds. *Standard:* Long and low with large head, narrow skull and well-developed peak. Sad expression with wrinkled loose skin covering head. Deeply sunken, sad, deep-brown eyes. Long, thin, velvety ears set low and folding over nose when drawn forward. Powerful neck and shoulders; short, heavy, powerful forelegs, muscu-

Ch. Rocky of Long View Acres is the outstanding son of the famous Ch. Siefenjagenheim Lazy Bones. This Basset is owned by Chris G. Teeter of Birmingham, Michigan.

lar barrel-shaped hindquarters. Large feet; dog must stand absolutely true on his feet. Chest deep, full and well ribbed. All hound colors.

No finer hunting companion can be found than the Basset Hound, an aristocratic breed of ancient lineage, originally raised by royalty for moderately slow hunting. His short legs enable him to penetrate dense underbrush. He is an intelligent hunting dog, loyal to his master. In fact, he is a one-man dog, when trained and handled only by his master, and will have nothing to do with anyone else under any circumstances. He is quite easy to control, and his sad, lugubrious expression is so exaggerated as to be comical and amusing. The Basset is very popular as a house pet.

BEAGLE

Size: Two sizes—either under 13" high or from 13" to 15" high. *Weight:* 18 to 30 pounds. *Standard:* Tight-fitting short coat that feels quite hard. Outstandingly long drooping ears, large sad soft eyes and slightly long, always wagging high-held tail. Muzzle straight and square-cut, medium length. Neck rising free and light from shoulders. The Beagle gives the appearance of a miniature Foxhound. Solid and big for his inches, not too heavy. Colors: usually tan and black with white.

Ch. Gaycroft Chuckle poses proudly as if for the show ring. This Beagle is owned by Mary Alice Ward and Louise M. Hoe of Maryward Kennels, North Babylon, New York.

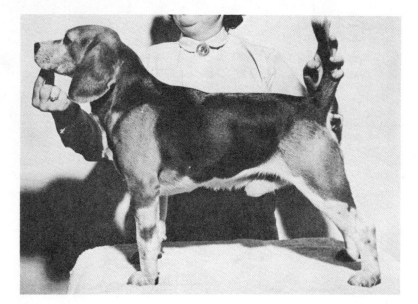

The Beagle is descended from the scent hounds used by King Arthur and his Knights of the Roundtable. He is still used only as a hunting dog in England. In America, however, he is a popular house pet. The earliest settlers of America brought their hounds with them and gradually refined the breed to produce the merry dog known as the Beagle. As a rabbit hunter, the Beagle alone or in packs is supreme. The Beagle is popular in city apartments and suburban yards but needs freedom of action outdoors.

BEDLINGTON TERRIER

Size: 15" to 16" high. *Weight:* 22 to 24 pounds. *Standard:* Soft but crisp 1"-long coat, topknot trimmed to give Roman-nosed appearance. Long tapering ears hang flat. Tail fairly long, tapered, carried gracefully. Colors: blue, liver, sandy and tan.

Aristocratic and distinguished in appearance, the Bedlington was bred originally in England to catch rats and draw badgers. He is a proud and spirited dog with a distinctive mincing gait. Women today have adopted the breed, and his old fierceness is now dormant, though his spirit is still evident when he fights for a place in his owner's affection.

Trimming the Bedlington is an art, but not difficult to learn from watching.

BEDLINGTON
Ch. Braemar Rascal is the son of Ch. Braemar Barney and Ch. Braemar Rose. Rascal was first shown when 10½ months old and acquired his championship within a month! Now retired, he was always a showman of fire and spirit. He is owned by Dorothy E. Morrison of Braemar Kennels, Chatham, New Jersey.

BELGIAN SHEEPDOG

Size: About 23″ high. *Weight:* 55 to 60 pounds. *Standard:* A big, upstanding dog with sturdy, straight legs and long tail carried low. Ears erect and muzzle moderately long and pointed. Thick, heavy coat is medium-long and lies close to the body. Color: black.

Up until July, 1959, several different varieties of dogs were classified under the single name, Belgian Sheepdog. At that time the A.K.C. decided that only the Groenendael, a black variety, would be recognized as the Belgian Sheepdog, while other former varieties would be recognized as separate breeds. His valuable contribution to police work and war work led to his importation into America.

BLOODHOUND

Size: Male, 25″ to 27″ high; female, 23″ to 25″ high. *Weight:* Male, 90 to 110 pounds; female, 80 to 100 pounds. *Standard:* Built powerfully, strong and long and well muscled, the larger and heavier the better. The Bloodhound's outstanding characteristic is his ability to scent. His expression is noble and dignified, giving an impression of solemnity, wisdom and power. Skull is long and narrow with pronounced occipital peak. Head is narrow in proportion to length and long in proportion to body so that it appears flattened at the sides. Eyes are deeply sunk and vary in color from deep hazel to yellow and lids are diamond-shaped. Ears thin and soft, extremely long, set very low and fall in graceful folds. Skin feels thin to touch and very loose so that it hangs in deep folds about the head and neck, forming a pronounced dewlap. Free and swinging gait. Colors: black and tan, red and tan, tawny; darker colors sometimes mixed with lighter or badger-colored hair, and sometimes flecked with white.

Unrivaled in his power to scent and to stick with a trail until the quarry is located, the purebred Bloodhound is also one of the most docile of breeds. He is so accurate in his trail that he is the only dog whose evidence is accepted in a court of law. Great Bloodhounds of America have brought about more convictions that some human detectives, one actually having convicted 600!

The Bloodhound's history is believed to extend back long before the Christian era. The Crusaders brought him to Europe from Constantinople. Bishops were among the first to develop the Bloodhound, as kennels were important parts of every monastery in those days, and they are credited with keeping the strain so clean that the hound came to be known as the "blooded hound," meaning aristocratic. However, several centuries later, a noted English physician and dog lover explained the name as deriving from the Bloodhound's unique ability to scent blood.

Robert Noerr of Stamford, Connecticut, owns Ch. Palomine of Idol Ours. Bloodhounds excel at trailing.

BORDER TERRIER

Size: Height at withers 12″ to 13″—slightly greater distance between tail and withers. *Weight:* 13 to 15½ pounds. *Standard:* General appearance intensely alive and alert, always triggered for action. Rough, wiry coat, keen eyes, "otter" shape to head. Small, dark, V-shaped ears which don't break above the level of the head. Short dark muzzle with a few whiskers. Forelegs straight, hindquarters muscular with long thighs; small compact feet with toes pointed forward. Colors: red; grizzle and tan; blue and tan; wheaten.

Bred for centuries as a working dog, this staunch, fearless terrier is a hard worker for his size. His legs are long enough to keep up with a horse, but short enough so that he is unsurpassed in running to earth the foxes which prey on livestock in the border country of his native England. He is a tireless hunter, and his thick coat makes him impervious to hours of drenching rains or mists. Elevated from a purely working dog to a show dog in England about 40 years ago, this breed is rising fast in popularity in America.

A happy dog is Int. Ch. Lucky Purchase, now retired to a life of hunting after winning her 12th Best of Breed in the United States. In 1951, at the age of 2, she was imported from England by her owner, Mrs. Harry H. Webb of Shelburne, Vermont.

Left: Ch. Rachmaninoff is white with gold spots. He was 8 when this picture was taken. On the right he is joined by Sascha of Baronoff, a 6-week-old Borzoi puppy. They are owned by Mrs. Katherine E. McCluskey, Baronoff Kennels, Wenonah, New Jersey.

BORZOI (Russian Wolfhound)

Size: 26″ to 31″ high. *Weight:* 60 to 105 pounds. *Standard:* Narrow and graceful body with long head, inclined to be Roman-nosed. Small drop ears, slanted eyes. Silky, medium-long coat with heavy neck frill, long feathered tail carried in a graceful curve. Colors: white with lemon, tan, brindle or black markings.

Formerly a dog of state for the Czars of Russia, the Borzoi is an animal of elegance and beauty. For many centuries these very fast dogs, working in pairs, were used to chase and catch wolves on the steppes of Russia. Seizing the quarry by the ears, they would hold it until the huntsmen arrived.

As a pet the Borzoi needs little care and attention. Many professional people choose him for a pet, if they can provide the space for the exercise the large Borzoi needs.

BOSTON TERRIER

Size: About 16″ high. *Weight:* 3 classes: under 15 pounds (lightweight); 15 to 20 pounds (middleweight); 20 but not exceeding 25 pounds (heavyweight). *Standard:* Square head, short nose, square body. Outstanding feature, erect ears. Large, round eyes. Short, satiny coat marked with white. Tail short, fine and tapering, carried higher than level of back. General appearance compactly built, well-balanced, lively and intelligent. Color: brindle evenly marked with white.

The Boston Terrier conveys an impression of determination, strength and activity. His carriage is easy and graceful. The breed was developed as an outgrowth of a mating in 1870 of a crossbred Bull Terrier or White English Terrier

owned by a Robert C. Hooper of Boston and a dog named Gyp or Kate owned by an Edward Burnett of Southboro, Mass. The female was white, weighed about 20 pounds and was of a bulldog type. All Boston Terriers are descendants of this match. At first the breed was called Round-Headed Bull Terrier but later was renamed Boston Terrier, for the match took place in Boston.

Great progress has been made in developing the breed with different strains and this has resulted in a clean-cut dog with a body approximating the conformation of a terrier rather than a bulldog.

The Boston, although not a fighter, is able to take care of himself. His gentle disposition has won him the name of The American Gentleman among dogs. He is eminently suitable as a companion and house pet.

BOUVIER DES FLANDRES

Size: 23″ to 27½″ high. *Weight:* About 70 to 95 pounds. *Standard:* Powerful, cobby dog, upstanding, short in back, compact but not heavy. Medium long head, ears erect when cropped. Rough coat of medium length, with mustache, beard and bushy eyebrows. Tail docked, usually carried up. Colors range from fawn to black, including brindle.

An uncommon breed in America today, the Bouvier des Flandres is making a heartening comeback after being nearly snuffed out by two World Wars which

These photographs taken by Nina Leen show Yhelot, the "grand old lady" of Fred H. Walsh's Deewal Kennels of Frenchtown, New Jersey. In 1956 she was the first Bouvier in 13 years to be shown in the Westminster Show! Two years later there were seven Bouviers entered in the Westminster, four of them her descendants. On the right she is shown with one of her granddaughters, Ch. Deewal Toronto.

devastated his native Flanders. This gallant working dog, bred to herd cattle, is strong and muscular, capable of withstanding the hardest work and most inclement weather. Trained for police and guard work, he brings all his tremendous energy and intelligence to bear, and is still used in Belgium for pulling small carts as well as for farm work. The Bouvier, while a fierce defender, is also exceptionally gentle and obedient. He makes a loyal family dog with a special liking for children.

BOXER

Size: Male, 22″ to 24″ high at withers; female, 21″ to 23″ high. *Weight:* Male, 66 pounds; female, 62 pounds (for given heights). *Standard:* Clean lines and elegant appearance, powerful muscles visibly rippling beneath short, shiny coat. Noble head, slightly rounded on top, strong undershot jaw, nose tilted up, ears clipped to a point and head wrinkled between ears when latter are held erect. Colors: fawn or brindle, possibly with some white markings; black mask on face required.

The Boxer is a cousin to almost all types of bulldogs and displays their usual courage and stamina. His ancestry dates back to old fighting dogs of Tibet. Other later ancestors of his were depicted in old tapestries. His appearance is

Int. Ch. Eldic's Dornis, 2½-year-old Boxer, owned by Eleanor Haeberle of Eldic Kennels, Basking Ridge, New Jersey.

regal both in repose and in action, with a proud carriage and a graceful stride. His high intelligence and fearlessness made him an ideal fighter of both dogs and bulls before such sports were outlawed. Those qualities today have led him to be trained for police work in Germany. His name, which is English despite his German development, stems from his habit of fighting with his front paws, somewhat like a man boxing.

In spite of his ferocious looks, the Boxer is a friendly and playful dog, a wonderful and popular pet and a fine show dog. His short, sleek coat makes him an easy dog to care for.

BRIARD

Size: 22" to 27" high. *Weight:* 70 to 80 pounds. *Standard:* Squarely built and powerful. Short back, head large and long with heavy hair falling over ears, eyes and muzzle. Ears semi-erect. Tail long, low and well-feathered. Coat long,

Right: Gilles de la Gaillarde is the black Briard shown here. Below: The tawny Briard is Forever Amber de la Gaillarde. Both dogs are owned by Gay Norgaard of Shell Beach, California.

slightly wavy and stiff in texture. Hind legs have double dewclaws. Colors: dark and mainly black, gray or tawny; also white.

This dog has been in America since Revolutionary times. He was originally brought from France where he worked as a sheep tender since the 12th century on the lonely hillsides, especially in the province of Brie.

Too large for an ordinary house dog, the Briard makes a fine show dog.

Ch. Piney Ridge Pixie, a Brittany Spaniel owned by Marshall Anderson of Lincoln Park, Michigan.

BRITTANY SPANIEL

Size: 17½" to 20½" high. *Weight:* 30 to 40 pounds. *Standard:* Compact, rugged and closely-knit build but so leggy that height at withers is same as body length. Straight and short back; broad, muscular hindquarters with powerful thighs and hip set well into the loin at angle which allows for powerful drive when in motion; fairly full, rounded flanks and strong loins. Sloping and muscular shoulders and deep chest, well-sprung ribs. Skull is rounded, rather wedge-shaped but evenly formed, with muzzle of medium length that tapers gradually to well-open nostrils which permit deep breathing and adequate scenting while at top speed. Lips tight to muzzle and dry so that feathers don't stick. Eyes set well in head and protected by heavy, expressive eyebrows. Short and leafy ears, set high, lie flat and close to head, lightly fringed but heavily covered with dense, rather short hair. Naturally tailless or docked not over 4". Coat is dense, flat or wavy but never curly and not as fine as in other spaniel breeds. Colors: dark orange and white, or liver and white. Light ticking.

Like all spaniels, pointers and setters, the basic stock of the Brittany Spaniel came from Spain but the greatest development of this breed took place in the British Isles. The first tailless ancestor of the modern Brittany Spaniel was bred about 100 years ago in Brittany, France. The lovely orange and white coloring of the present-day Brittany Spaniel was developed early in the 20th century by a Frenchman who crossed pointers with the spaniel to achieve this coloring and yet retain keen scenting ability. Strong, vigorous, energetic and quick of movement, he makes an excellent hunting companion and is unique as a spaniel that points game. He has a gentle disposition, is wonderful as a children's pet, and is small enough for city dwelling.

BRUSSELS GRIFFON

Size: About 8″ high. *Weight:* 5 to 12 pounds. *Standard:* Short, compact and sturdy body stands on straight legs. But the head is the distinguishing feature of the Griffon—large, with a broad domed skull and pronounced stop, very flat face, short, tipped-up nose, broad muzzle, black wide nostrils—all set off by bushy eyebrows, whiskers and cheek fringes. Undershot jaw has definite upsweep and lips come together neatly, showing neither teeth nor tongue. Expressive and very dark and large eyes. Ears are semi-erect. Tail held high and cut ⅓. Colors: reddish-brown, black, or black with reddish-brown markings.

There are three varieties of the Griffon, though all are the same breed and appear in the same litters. The Brussels Griffon has a rough red coat, coarse and wiry like a terrier's, with profuse beard and whiskers. The Belgian Griffon (also known as Belge) is identical except for the color—black, black and tan, or a mixture of black and tan hairs which appear brownish rather than clear red as

Three Brussels Griffon puppies from the Barmere Kennels of Mrs. William Z. Breed of Bel-Air, Los Angeles, California. The center pup is Ch. Barmere's I'm a Pixie, a champion at 10 months.

in the Brussels. The Petit Brabancon (or smooth-coated Griffon) resembles the other two except for the coat which is close and smooth like a Boxer's and the colors may be deep red with black mask or black and tan. (Also see *Griffon, Wire-haired Pointing.*)

Sometimes called the "Doggiest of Toy Dogs," the Brussels Griffon is a distinctive and unusual dog with none of the pampered toy dog about him. From the tip of his turned-up nose to the end of his gaily carried tail, he is all jaunty good humor and still retains a delightful Belgian street urchin quality about him. The Griffon developed from the crossing of the Belgian street dog and the Affenpinscher, Pug and Ruby Spaniel, and was at one time used to kill stable vermin. It was from the Ruby Spaniel that he inherited his unique and appealing facial characteristics but because of this strain, he is no longer able to do the stable work he was once so well suited for. He is an excellent watch-dog and his lively personality, super-intelligence, affection and devotion add to his appeal as a wonderful pet. However, he is quite sensitive and shy with strangers, and although obedient and easily managed, the Griffon tends some-times to be difficult to break in with the leash so it's wise to start this training very early. He's a comrade on hikes and in swimming.

Although fierce in appearance, the Bulldog is a gentle, affectionate animal. The dog pictured is about to become a mother.

BULLDOG

Size: About 15" high. *Weight:* 40 to 50 pounds. *Standard:* Heavy thick-set, low-slung body. Massive, short-faced head, wide shoulders and sturdy limbs. Head broad, face wrinkled, ears small, thick and folding in and backward. Tail short. General appearance of great stability, vigor and strength. Gait loose-jointed, shuffling sidewise with characteristic roll. Short, smooth coat. Colors: red brindle, other brindles, solid white, solid red, fawn or fallow, piebald; in brindles and solid colors, small white patch on chest not detrimental.

Prior to the outlawing of the sport in England, the Bulldog, originally a very ferocious animal, was used for bull-baiting. His low-slung body protected him somewhat from the thrusts of the bull.

Today's Bulldog has a beauty and symmetry of form along with extraordinary courage. His short nose and long heavy underjaw make the Bulldog a symbol for determination.

BULL-MASTIFF

Size: 24" to 27" high. *Weight:* 100 to 115 pounds. *Standard:* Strong, muscular and symmetrical body, with slightly arched neck almost equal in circumference to skull; wide and deep chest, well-sprung ribs, muscular shoulders, loins and hind legs. Large and square skull with fair wrinkle, circumference measures almost height of dog. Deep and broad muzzle, with large nostrils but not too pendulous flews and large canine teeth set wide. V-shaped ears carried close to cheek or folded back, set wide and high, giving a square appearance to the skull. Short and dense coat gives good weather protection. Tail set high up, strong at root and tapering, reaching to the hocks, carried straight or curved. Colors: any shade of fawn or brindle, white, red, piebald.

Fearless, powerful and alert, the Bull-Mastiff was tailor-made to serve the needs of 19th century English gamekeepers who were having a great deal of difficulty keeping poachers away from the large estates and game preserves they watched over. They needed a dog with the power and courage of the Mastiff but he wasn't fast or aggressive enough. The Bulldog, who was big, strong and active in those days, was a bit too ferocious and not large enough. The gamekeepers wanted dogs that would remain silent at the approach of poachers, would attack on command, but would not maul the intruders, just throw them. By crossing the Mastiff and Bulldog, they produced just the dog they needed, the Bull-Mastiff, called "Gamekeeper's Night-Dog" in those days. His development was wholly a utilitarian one, but sometimes he was used in contests or demonstrations, muzzled and with a club-carrying man as adversary. The Bull-Mastiff was always the winner in such contests.

From England, interest in the breed spread to Siam, India, Malaya, Africa and America. His short coat protects him from the sun in hot countries and yet his strength enables him to endure all kinds of bad weather. Despite his fearlessness which makes him an ideal guardian of home and property, the Bull-Mastiff is docile and loyal.

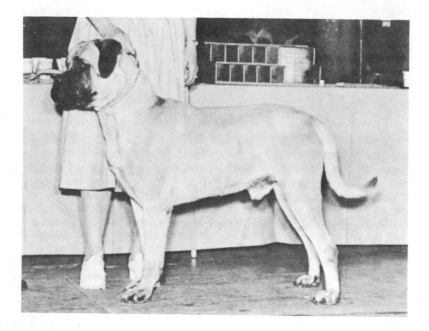

Here is one of the finest Bull-Mastiffs, both an American and Canadian champion. He is owned by Mr. and Mrs. C. D. Hurst of Hurstacres Kennels, Muncie, Indiana.

Ch. Kowhai Uncle Bimbo is a colored Bull Terrier, as fine a specimen of the breed as can be found in America. He is owned by Mr. and Mrs. Alfred T. Bibby of the Holcroft Kennels, Lynnfield, Massachusetts.

BULL TERRIER

Size: 19″ to 22″ high. *Weight:* 40 to 60 pounds. *Standard:* Short but strong, muscular body, sturdy straight legs. Long head of unbroken line, no step down from skull to muzzle. Short, erect ears and small slanting eyes. Thick, short, smooth coat, normally white but may be colored, usually brindle with white. Short, straight tail carried stiffly away from body but not above back level.

The Bull Terrier was bred over 100 years ago from the Bulldog and the now-extinct white English Terrier. He quickly became one of the most fashionable fighting dogs of England but since then he has become a gentle dog, gay, lovable and friendly unless provoked. He makes a fine guard for children and property. He can be used as a hunting or herding dog, and pound for pound he is probably the strongest breed of dog today.

Perfect examples of the distinctive Cairn Terrier head and personality are these two 5-month-old puppies owned by Lydia S. Coleman, Wolfpit Kennels, Sharon, Connecticut.

CAIRN TERRIER

Size: 9″ or 10″ high. *Weight:* 13 to 14 pounds. *Standard:* A shaggy, short-legged terrier with an exceptionally broad well-furred face and foxy expression. Ears small, triangular and erect and short-haired. Coat rough and hard with dense undercoat. Frisky tail, furred but not feathered. Any color but white.

Like other terriers, the Cairn is a hunter of vermin, in this case particularly among the cairns or rock piles of his native Isle of Skye. In appearance, however, the Cairn Terrier's head is distinctive and unique, with a blunt but varminty look, furriness, lashes and eyebrows. He is a tireless, active, agile little fellow with a merry disposition.

CHESAPEAKE BAY RETRIEVER

Size: 21″ to 26″ high; length from back of head to tail base, 34″ to 35″. *Weight:* Male, 65 to 75 pounds; female, 55 to 65 pounds. *Standard:* Most important is the texture of the coat which is oily in the harsh outer coat and woolly in the undercoat to prevent cold water from reaching the dog's skin and to aid in quick drying. A Chesapeake's coat resists the water in the same way that a duck's feathers do; when he leaves the water and shakes himself, his coat will not hold water at all. Color is also extremely important as in hunting it must be nearly that of the surroundings; any color varying from dark brown to faded tan or dead grass (dull straw) will qualify a dog for show. Legs straight, feet webbed, head broad, ears hang loosely, tail long and quite thick.

In the year 1807, two Newfoundland puppies were rescued from a wrecked English ship by an American ship. The two dogs were found to possess wonderful qualities as retrievers. It was not known exactly how these dogs were crossed but it seems possible that they were crossed with either an English Otter Hound or the Flat-coated and Curly-coated Retrievers. The rescued dogs landed in Maryland and the breed was developed along the shores of Chesapeake Bay. They developed a reputation for prowess in the rough icy waters of that bay and were eventually famous for their duck hunting, retrieving as many as 200 or 300 ducks in a day.

Sassie is owned by Mrs. Earl K. Ward, Fort Smith, Arkansas. Chesapeakes have great water aptitude.

An armful of Chihuahuas in the loving arms of their breeder, Marge Belden of North Madison, Ohio. Belden's La Grando Kid on the left and Belden's Tammy La Grando in the center are littermates. Ch. Belden's Miss America is owned by Mrs. Beatrice Hatch of Denver, Colorado.

CHIHUAHUA

Size: The more diminutive, the better. *Weight:* From 1 to 6 pounds, with 2 to 4 pounds most desirable. *Standard:* Well-rounded "apple dome" skull, somewhat pointed nose; large flaring ears with wide space in between; wide-set eyes, dark, ruby or luminous but light eyes in blond types. Lean shoulders well up to give soundness and balance. Hocks muscular and well apart. Tail carried up or out, or looped over the back but never tucked under; some born with no tail or a bobtail. Feet dainty and small. Smooth-coat variety soft in texture, close fitting and glossy. Long-coat variety soft and undercoated; fringed ears, large neck ruff, feathered feet and legs and long plume tail. Colors run the gamut from light to dark with splashing or markings or solid colors.

The Chihuahua is a Mexican dog whose ancestor, the Techichi, was probably from Central America. The little dogs were popular among the Toltecs and later the Aztecs, and archaeologists have found Chihuahuas buried in human graves. Another ancestor is believed to have been a small hairless dog which came to North America from China across a land bridge to Alaska.

This tiny dog makes an intelligent and lively pet. He is fond of humans but aloof and clannish as far as other dogs are concerned. He will have nothing to do with other breeds, but will mingle freely with his own elite brethren.

CHOW CHOW

Size: 19″ to 20″ in height. *Weight:* 50 to 60 pounds. *Standard:* Large and massive head in proportion to size of dog, with relatively short but broad muzzle set off by a ruff; large black nose and strong teeth with a scissors bite. Only breed in the world possessing a blue-black tongue. Almond-shaped dark eyes and small, round-tipped ears carried stiffly. Body short and compact, muscular and broad chest, powerful loins. Tail sets well up, carried close to the back. Compact, round catlike feet with thick pads. Massive, cobby, powerful dog with a lordly, almost arrogant expression on his face, and a completely individual gait, independent, aloof. Abundant coat, straight and off-standing, rather coarse-textured but with a soft, woolly undercoat. Color: any clear color (black, red, fawn or blue), solid throughout, with lighter shadings on ruff, tail, and breechings.

The breed is more than 2000 years old, but it is believed that the Chow existed even before that time and is one of the oldest recognizable types of dog. Chinese emperors had lavish kennels of Chows, and for centuries they were

Below: 6-week-old "Pagemoor's Brenda" owned and bred by Mr. and Mrs. Frederic R. Humpage, Pagemoor Chow Chow Kennels, North Wilbraham, Massachusetts, looks like a fat toy teddy bear.

Ch. Pagemoor's Blue Bunting, also owned by Mr. and Mrs. Frederic R. Humpage.

the principal sporting dogs, ideal as such for their powerful scenting powers, staunchness on point and clever hunting tactics. Amusingly, their name, Chow Chow, did not originate from China but from 18th century English masters of sailing vessels who described their various items of cargo from the Orient—later including these dogs—simply as "chow chow." The Chow, imported from England, made its debut in the United States in 1890, and today is firmly established in both countries as a companion, house and guard dog, appreciated for his cleanliness (no odor or fleas cling to him), affection and understanding.

COCKER SPANIEL

Size: About 14" high. *Weight:* Not under 22 nor over 28 pounds. *Standard:* Serviceable-looking dog with refined chiseled head. Straight legs. Body compact and wide. Tail docked. Eyes very soft and appealing in expression. Ears long and silky. Slightly wavy coat, soft with heavy feathering on ears, chest, underbody and legs (English Cocker larger, longer in head, and less heavily feathered than American: also heavier, weighing 26 to 34 pounds). Colors: black, black and tan, liver, shades of red and blond, parti-color with white.

Spaniels generally originated in Spain where they were used to assist hunters of birds. A good spaniel approached the wild birds from one side while hunters approached from the other. The smaller the spaniel, the better—as it could come closer to the game without being seen or heard. The Cocker is the smallest of the sporting spaniels, and was used in England to hunt woodcock. In 1859, at a dog show in Birmingham, England, the first Cocker was entered in competition. The Cocker has a smaller, more setter-like body than the other spaniels.

Over the years as the strain was developed, it became more popular. The Cocker's expression makes him most appealing as a pet and today he is used as much in the city as in the country. In America he is either the first or second dog in popularity year after year.

His English cousin is only slightly different in appearance.

Regular grooming keeps the Cocker neat and clean, with his long silky coat free of snarls.

A golden sable Collie, Ch. Conrad's Music Maestro, owned by Roy Ayers of Stone Mountain, Georgia. His sire was Ch. Poplar Stop the Music and his dame, Ch. Conrad Sweet Expression.

COLLIE

Size: 22" to 26" high at the shoulder. *Weight:* About 50 to 75 pounds. *Standard:* Long heavy coat and mane and frill. Proud carriage and light gait. Head long and slender. Eyes almond-shaped and slanted. Ears half-raised and turning to the front. Legs straight and strong. Body just a trifle longer than high. Long tail carried low with slight upward twist. Colors: sable and white, blue merle and white, or tricolor.

The Collie comes from the Scottish Highlands where he guarded the sheep. Possibly his name comes from the word colley, meaning black-faced sheep. In any event, he is one of the oldest of the shepherd dogs and appears often in literature. The Smooth Collie is rare; most Collies are Rough (that is, long-haired). The Shetland Sheepdog (see page 110) is a small-sized Collie.

He makes a fine pet and is a picture of grace as he romps around the yard. Quiet and easy to care for, he is an aristocrat.

COONHOUND (Black and Tan)

Size: Male, 24" to 26" high; female, 22" to 24" high. *Weight:* 50 to 60 pounds. *Standard:* Well-proportioned build, neither leggy nor close to ground. Level, powerful back, muscular shoulders and hindquarters, long and tapering stern. Chest well let down to form a deep keel between forelegs. Narrow, cleanly-modelled head with well-developed flews (upper lips) hanging down in typical hound fashion. Eyes not too deeply set. Ears set low on high-domed head, hanging in graceful folds. Large-boned forelegs. Short, thick coat. Long tail carried high when trailing. Colors: jet black with rich tan markings.

Compared to other purebreds, the Black and Tan Coonhound is a relative

Left: Coonhounds in action! They've treed a quarry and one "barks up" to alert their master, Mr. Don H. Stringer of The Hemphill Creek Hounds, Waynesville, North Carolina. Below: 14-week-old Black and Tan Coonhound, lovably gawky and padded with puppy fat, hardly resembles the sleek hunter he'll grow up to be. He is also owned and bred by Mr. Stringer.

newcomer, but his breed goes back to the Talbot hound of the 11th century, the Bloodhound and the Virginia Foxhound, often called the "black and tan." He was selectively bred over the years on the basis of color (as there were "cooners" of other colors) and for skill in trailing and treeing possum and raccoon (for which he is named). He can also be used for hunting deer, bear, bobcat, mountain lion, and other big game. Unlike the Foxhound, Harrier, or other hound breeds, the Coonhound trails entirely by scent, with nose to the ground, "barking up" or giving voice the minute he trees his quarry.

Powerful, agile and alert, he covers ground with strong rhythmic strides and can withstand any extremes of weather and the hardest terrain. Yet, in spite of his aggressiveness, he's friendly, eager and, of course, ever alert.

This female Dachshund is comfortable in her own basket. She is owned by Lois Meistrell of Great Neck Dog Training Center, Great Neck, Long Island, N. Y.

DACHSHUND

Three coat varieties—Smooth or Short-haired; Wire-haired; Long-haired. *Size:* 5″ to 9″ high. *Weight:* Standard, 9 to 20 pounds; Miniature, between 7.7 and 8.8 pounds at minimum age of 12 months. *Standard:* Short-legged, long-bodied, low to ground; sturdy, well-muscled, neither clumsy nor slim, with daring carriage and intelligent expression. The three varieties are similar in all respects except coat. Tapered head is broad, long and drooping. Forelegs not quite straight, feet turned slightly out. Tail not docked, fairly long, carried out from body but not high. Miniature exactly like Standard except for size. Colors: red, shades of tan, black and tan, chocolate, dappled, tiger and gray.

The Dachshund is a member of the hound group, his name meaning badger hound. In Europe he was used for centuries to hunt the rabbit and badger. His short, easily folded legs and long body with elastic skin make him useful for digging into burrows. The long head with powerful jaw was for fighting prey.

As a pet, the Dachshund is independent and sometimes stubborn. He makes his home readily with a family and is suitable for city life as well as outdoor running. The Dachshund is clever and quick in learning and can be a charming and enjoyable companion, especially when properly trained. The Dachshund is clean, small and has no doggy odor.

DALMATIAN

Size: 19" to 23" high. *Weight:* 35 to 50 pounds. *Standard:* Head of fair length, muzzle long as possible, lips clean, eyes rimmed with black in black-spotted dogs and with brown in liver-spotted dogs, moderately well apart but with intelligent expression. Ears set rather high and wide, gradually tapering to a rounded point and carried close to the head. Tail moderately long, carried with slight upward curve. Coat short, hard, dense and fine, neither woolly nor silky. Colors: most important that the Dalmatian has a white ground color; two varieties, black-spotted and liver-spotted, spots not intermingling but round and distinct.

The Dalmatian is traditionally associated with firemen as he will run with or ride on fire engines. Originally he came from the Austrian province of Dalmatia where he may have descended from an Italian pointer some 300 years

Standing perfectly still, the "fire dog" is the picture of pride and dignity.

ago. Originally a hunting dog, his love of running under carriages as guard and companion gained him the nickname of Coach Dog and from there to Fire Dog was just a step. It is possible that the Dalmatian stemmed from the Great Dane. He was an early favorite of wandering gypsy bands and is today a popular breed in suburban homes. He has a retentive memory and has been used for clowning in circuses and on the stage. The Dalmatian is picturesque and aristocratic in bearing, a gentleman, a quiet chap and an ideal guard dog, distinguishing nicely between barking for fun and with purpose. His courtesy never fails with visitors that he approves.

This handsome Dandie Dinmont Terrier is Ch. Overhill Conquistador sired by Ch. Waterbeck Watermark and dammed by Overhill Lynn. Her owners are Mr. and Mrs. William M. Kirby of Kansas City, Missouri.

DANDIE DINMONT TERRIER

Size: 8" to 11" high at top of shoulder, with body length no more than twice the height, preferably an inch or two shorter. *Weight:* 14 to 24 pounds, best weight around 18 pounds. *Standard:* Strong head covered with very fine silky hair, light in color; darker shade, heavier hair on muzzle, similar to feathers on forelegs. Strong, punishing teeth with the upper teeth slightly overlapping. Eyes wide-set, low and prominent, dark in color. Pendulous ears set low with thin feather matching hair of topknot. Coat mixture of hard and soft hair. Hair on underbelly softer and lighter. Tail feathers taper to a point. Colors: pepper or mustard colored.

There is probably no breed of dog with a more literary name than the Dandie Dinmont Terrier. This dog was bred along the border between England and Scotland and specialized in hunting the otter and badger. Sir Walter Scott gave it its name indirectly when, in *Guy Mannering*, he lovingly described the six little terriers owned by a farmer named Dandie Dinmont.

The Dandie makes an excellent pet and is adaptable as far as space is concerned. He is equally happy in large outdoor environments and in a small city apartment, where his small size is belied by his large-dog temperament. He also makes an excellent show dog, because he can be shown in his natural state without clipping, needing only daily brushing and combing, with special attention to the topknot and points of the ears, which fluff up to form the dog's most characteristic feature.

An outstanding Doberman, a Best in Show winner, is Ch. Dortmund Delly's Colonel Jet, owned by Natalie Stebbins of Westbury, Long Island, N. Y.

DOBERMAN PINSCHER

Size: 24″ to 28″ high. *Weight:* 60 to 75 pounds. *Standard:* Good middle-sized dog with square body, compactly built, muscular and powerful. Great endurance in speed. Proud carriage, energetic. Head long and rather wedge-shaped. Ears small, carried erect when cropped. Eyes almond-shaped, not round. Back short, tail docked. Smooth hard coat fits close to skin. Good reach in forequarters when running and good driving power in hindquarters. Colors: black, brown or blue.

One man, Herr Louis Dobermann, the dog catcher of a small German town, is responsible for this unusual breed. Pinscher in German means terrier, and this breed is probably descended from terrier-type dogs. Herr Dobermann founded the breed in 1890 by crossing the German Shepherd, Rottweiler and Old English Terrier.

Renowned as an outstanding war and police dog, the Doberman is clean of line throughout. Bold and alert, he is courageous in war, gallant at home, a gentleman, an affectionate and obedient pet. An intelligent dog with natural working ability, he needs training to reach his peak as a house pet.

Not recognized in the United States until 1908, he has been adopted as the official dog of the U.S. Marine Corps and has served as a sentry and trailing dog.

(See photo on previous page.)

Lovely and lovable, Ch. Scyld's The Black Widow stands at the point. Mr. and Mrs. Elsworth Howell of Betsworth Kennels, Darien, Connecticut, are the owners of this ideal English Setter.

ENGLISH SETTER

Size: 23″ to 25″ high. *Weight:* 50 to 70 pounds. *Standard:* Head long and lean, with long and deep muzzle, and alert dark eyes. Silky ears droop low. Long, flat and beautifully feathered coat. Long fringed tail tapers to a point at the tip and is carried straight out. Colors: white with black, tan, blue, lemon, orange and liver belton markings, or solid white.

The English Setter probably had its origin some 400 years ago, produced from crosses of the Spanish Pointer, Water Spaniel and Springer Spaniel. Intensive and intelligent breeding has produced the increasingly popular dog we know today. The beauty of the English Setter is more than skin deep. His intelligence, personality and sweet nature make this rugged outdoor dog an ideal companion in the field or in the country home.

ENGLISH SHEPHERD

Size: 18" to 23" high. *Weight:* 40 to 60 pounds. *Standard:* (not A.K.C.) Medium-sized working dog, alert and intelligent. Medium-long head, moderately defined stop, skull broad and slightly rounded, tapering muzzle, powerful jaws, nose solid black, dark slightly oblique eyes, ears wide at base, lying close to head folded over near top. Horizontal back, straight legs, moderately long plume-like tail. Abundant coat with long rather coarse straight or wavy hair, soft undercoat. Colors: black and tan, tricolor, sable and white, black and white.

Working cattle is the primary function of the English Shepherd and he is judged both for his ability to handle cattle in the field and for type, balance, soundness, gait and temperament. He possesses agility, stamina and stouthearted perseverance and combines a natural instinct for his work with a willingness to obey his master. English Shepherds are not registered in the American Kennel Club nor shown in their dog shows.

Right: Halsell's Roger is an exceptionally fine specimen of an English Shepherd. Below: Roger is shown in action turning cattle on a farm. Roger is owned by Fulwar S. Halsell, Comdr. U. S. N., Ret., breeder and trainer, of Edwardsburg, Michigan.

Ch. Tahquitz Solita and her litter of 5 champions sired by Ch. Melilotus Royal Oak. Breeder of the Springers is Juanita Waite Howard of Waiterock Ranch, Lafayette, California.

ENGLISH SPRINGER SPANIEL

Size: 18″ to 18½″ high. *Weight:* Male, 45 to 50 pounds; female, 42 to 47 pounds. *Standard:* Nostrils well developed, muzzle deep, jaws fairly square, skull of medium length and fairly broad. Eyebrows and temple well developed; long, wide ears. Chest deep and well developed. Legs straight from shoulder to foot. Fine glossy coat with a nice fringe on the throat, brisket, chest and belly. Colors: liver and white; black and white; liver and tan; black and tan; tan and white; black, white and tan; liver; black; roan.

The Springer has a gait that is strictly his own. His four legs swing forward from the shoulder in a free and easy manner, rolling his feet well forward and showing that he is a hunting dog with speed, agility and endurance. He is a gentle, companionable dog, a joy to the family as well as to the hunter.

Ch. Stella of Laoi, a Prince Charles, in a pose showing the appeal of these little Spaniels when they gaze at a loved human. Owner and breeder: Miriam O. Goodridge of Egypt, Massachusetts.

ENGLISH TOY SPANIEL
(King Charles, Prince Charles, Ruby and Blenheim)

Size: About 10″ high. *Weight:* Small as 6 pounds, but most desirable, 9 to 12 pounds. *Standard:* Well-domed, semiglobular head with wide-set eyes, large and dark—stop or hollow between the eyes is well marked and deep enough to bury a small marble. Pert turned-up nose, black and wide, with open nostrils. Wide lower jaws also turn up and conceal the teeth. Long (20—22″), it has heavily-feathered ears hang flat to sides of cheeks. Short, compact and cobby body covered by long, silky, wavy but not curly, hair. Profuse mane extends well down in front of chest, and feet so thickly feathered they look webbed. Tail cut to about 1½″ from 3″ to 4″ is also feathered and carried to level of the back. Colors: vary with the variety—King Charles (Black and Tan) is rich glossy black and deep mahogany tan; Prince Charles White, in addition. Ruby is a rich chestnut red and whole-colored. Blenheim is pure pearly white with bright deep chestnut or ruby red markings evenly distributed in large patches.

The affectionate, intelligent little English Toy Spaniel was the darling of English royalty, aristocrats and the wealthy for at least three centuries, as the names of the varieties indicate. Authorities believe he originated in Japan or

China, came to Spain and thence to England. There is also a story that specimens of this toy breed were presented to King James I by the emperor of Japan, whose royal presents always included dogs. In any event, the Toy Spaniel won the hearts of English court people and when Mary, Queen of Scots was executed, her little Toy Spaniel refused to leave her, even on the scaffold. The Black and Tan variety was the first to appear, and the other varieties, distinguished by color (but identical in other respects) developed later. For a long time they were bred without any reference to color, often the same litter producing several varieties, but in modern times, the science of color breeding set the different varieties apart.

The English Toy Spaniel makes an intelligent, deeply devoted and perceptive companion whose hunting instincts are still evident.

ESKIMO (Spitz)

Size: Male, 22″ to 25″ high; female, 20″ to 23″ high. *Weight:* Male, 65 to 85 pounds; female, 50 to 70 pounds. *Standard:* Powerful jaws, eyes small and deep-set, ears short and firm, carried erect and turned forward. Tail large and bushy. All known colors.

The Eskimo dog, one of the world's best work dogs, originated in Greenland, Labrador and other Arctic regions. Smaller breeds which have borrowed his name were at one time known as Spitz. Because this dog is so intelligent, he has often been trained for the circus, performing such tricks as walking on

Mother and puppies of an American Eskimo family owned by the Rev. and Mrs. Virgil T. Stout of Mell-o-Bark Kennels, Alvordton, Ohio.

tightropes. Mostly, however, the Eskimo has been used for pulling sleds for North Pole explorers and inhabitants of the Arctic. The Eskimo can stand both cold weather and hot and has a self-cleaning coat. His keen nose makes him a fine hunting assistant.

As a pet, the Eskimo is affectionate when fairly treated, fine with children but rather pugnacious when with other breeds or animals. He rarely makes a sound but when he does, he generally does not bark but yelps or howls like a wolf.

This alert English Foxhound is owned by Denison B. Hull of Chicago, Illinois.

FOXHOUND (English and American)

Size: 23" to 24" high at the withers; females 1" shorter. *Weight:* Male, 80 to 90 pounds; female, 10 pounds lighter. *Standard:* Head fairly long with straight square-cut muzzle, drop-ears set low, their tips being rounded, eyes very soft in expression. Body long, strong and muscular, legs straight as a post, tail carried gaily. The American Foxhound is slightly less sturdy in build than the English variety. Colors: black, tan and white; all white; and shades of buff or gray.

No animal with the exception of the racehorse has had so much effort and money devoted to its breeding as the English Foxhound. In order to hunt the fox in the traditional English fashion, the hound must have a keen nose, a good voice, a determination to reach its quarry and the stamina to run as far as 100 miles a day, 2 or 3 days a week at speeds often reaching 30 miles an hour. Since breeding a working pack (perhaps 60) of English Foxhounds is so great a task, the masters look with disfavor on using the dogs for anything but hunting. In spite of their aristocratic appearance, they are almost never seen at dog shows.

FOX TERRIER (Smooth and Wire-haired)

Size: 14½″ to 15½″ high. *Weight:* 15 to 19 pounds. *Standard:* Generally gay, lively and active. Neither leggy nor too short of leg. Skull flat and moderately narrow, gradually decreasing in width to the eyes. Ears V-shaped and small. Jaws strong and muscular. Eyes and rims dark in color. Docked tail

Fox Terriers are known for their great balancing ability, and the smooth Fox Terrier here seems to be enjoying his performance.

The Wire-haired Fox Terrier is Ch. Edswyre Supermaid, owned by Mrs. Mabel Farr.

stands up straight. Smooth coat differs only in that coat is quite thick but short and hard, while Wire-haired is longer, broken and wiry. Colors: white predominating with markings of black or black and tan.

The Fox Terrier is an ancient breed of English origin. The Smooth variety antedated the Wire by some 15 to 20 years in the show ring and is said to be a descendant of the rough-coated working terrier of Wales, while the ancestors of the Smooth were the Bull Terrier, Greyhound and Beagle.

Because of his keen nose, remarkable eyesight and staying powers, the Fox Terrier drives the fox from his hole when closely pursued by the hounds.

Both varieties are used today not only for hunting but as house pets. They have been interbred in order to give the cleaner-cut head and more classical outlines of the Smooth to the Wire, but interbreeding has now been discontinued.

FRENCH BULLDOG

Size: About 12" high. *Weight:* 18 to 28 pounds. *Standard:* Rather heavily built, short well-rounded body, broad in front. Large square-shaped head with short broad muzzle and eyes set wide apart. Ears unique—stiffly carried, with opening directly forward, broad at the base and rounded at top. Naturally short tail may be straight or screw. Smooth and glossy short-hair coat. Color: brindle, fawn, white or brindle and white.

English in origin, French by adoption, the French Bulldog owes to America the preservation of its distinctive appearance! The erect, bat-shaped ears would otherwise have been bred out in favor of the rose ear, making the dog a sort of miniature English Bulldog. The desired expression on the face of an ideal "Frenchie" is bright and alert, unlike the rather pugnacious expression of his English cousin.

As a pet, he makes an excellent companion and trustworthy watchdog. His small size, short hair and sweet, quiet disposition make him an excellent choice for an indoor pet. He seldom barks, but is a fun-loving, frolicsome pet.

Ch. Montgomery's Petit Jeeper weighed 19 pounds at the age of 2 when this picture was taken. This French Bulldog is owned by Mrs. Sara B. Montgomery of Harrisburg, Penna.

The magnificent stance of the German Shepherd is completely, dynamically balanced. At rest as well as in motion, he is a picture of alertness. The dog pictured here is owned by Julius Due of Huntington Station, New York.

GERMAN SHEPHERD

Size: 23″ to 25″ high. *Weight:* 16 to 85 pounds. *Standard:* Strong, agile, well-muscled animal, alert and full of life. Dog is longer than tall. Deep-bodied. Direct, fearless but not hostile expression. Double coat, the amount of under-coat varying with the season. Outer coat dense, hair straight, harsh and lying close to the body. A trotting dog, gait seeming effortless. Body gracefully rounded, chest deep, legs straight, head clean-cut, muzzle wedge-shaped, jaws strong. Long pointed ears stand erect. Long tail carried with slight curve. Colors: commonly black and tan, gray or black.

Probably the most international of all breeds, the German Shepherd's original home, Germany, gave him his name. In England the dog was called an Alsatian. Because he is often used as a police dog, German Police is a misnomer applied to the breed. Another misconception, caused by the wolf-gray color and general outline of the German Shepherd, is that he is closely related to the wolf. This is true only insofar as all dogs are descended from a common ancestor with wolves. In fact, German Shepherd dogs guard flocks and herds against wolves.

The German Shepherd is not a breed to make immediate and indiscriminate friendships. In living with a family, the dog gains confidence and soon becomes a fit and willing companion, watchdog, leader of the blind, baby sitter, and guardian.

GOLDEN RETRIEVER

Size: 20½″ to 24″ high. *Weight:* 55 to 70 pounds. *Standard:* Coat dense and water-repellent with good undercoat. Texture not as hard as a short-hair dog nor silky as a setter. Moderate feathering. Outstanding characteristic is lustrous golden color of various shades. Coat can be flat or wavy. Body deep and rather short. Tail long, straight and feathered. Head broad, muzzle powerful, eyes dark and wide apart. Ears medium-sized and dropped. Powerful, active dog, not clumsy nor long in leg, displaying kindly expression. Color: golden.

Primarily a hunting dog, the Golden Retriever possesses a personality that is eager, alert and self-confident. He should be kept in hard working condition.

The Golden Retriever is derived from hardy Russian stock. In 1860, a member of the English nobility visited a circus in Brighton, England, and saw a troupe of Russians with performing dogs called Russian Trackers. The Eng-

Although the Golden Retriever wins many awards for his beauty, he is a true hunting dog, happiest at the work he's been bred and trained for.

lishman, who was later to become the first Lord Tweedmouth, bought and raised the eight dogs. Later he crossed them with the Bloodhound. With the increased scenting powers from the Bloodhound the breed, already possessed of high intelligence and the ability to withstand cold weather and rigorous living, became more valuable. The size was reduced, the texture of the coat refined. The cross was made once only.

The Golden Retriever's forte is retrieving. He is equally at home on land and in water. He may be used simply as a retriever or as a combined setter and retriever. First brought to America just before World War I, the Golden Retriever, although once rare, is becoming very popular.

Gordon Setter Ch. Valiant Captain of East Court is owned by George W. von Osthoff, Staatsburg, New York.

GORDON SETTER

Size: Male, 24″ to 27″ high; female, 23″ to 26″ high. *Weight:* Male, 55 to 75 pounds; female, 45 to 65 pounds. *Standard:* Good-sized, sturdily built dog, well muscled. Strong, rather short back. Well-sprung ribs, short tail. Fairly heavy head. Noble, dignified expression. Coat straight or slightly waved but soft and shiny resembling silk. Colors: deep shining coal black with tan markings, a rich chestnut or mahogany red color.

Named for the Duke of Gordon in Scotland, this is a sturdy hunter capable of doing a full day's work in the field, with a characteristic aim to work for a loving master. Beauty, brains and bird sense are his outstanding traits. The

Gordon Setter came into prominence in the kennels of the 4th Duke of Gordon in the late 1700's. He is not a fast dog but has good staying power. The dog was imported into America by Daniel Webster in 1842.

The owner of a Gordon Setter possesses a rare combination—an aristocrat of rich beauty, a shooting companion of keen intelligence, a loyal family guard and a most pettable dog. The Gordon is not the pal of every passerby but loves being near his owners. His gentleness with children is a byword. Occasionally he is aggressive with other dogs who enter his province.

GREAT DANE

Size: Male, not less than 30″, preferably over 32″ high; female, 2 inches shorter in height. *Weight:* 120 to 150 pounds. *Standard:* Large, imposing dog with long, narrow, finely-chiseled head and deep, square muzzle. Dark, bright eyes, ears drooping forward close to cheeks, or cropped and erect. Short back and straight legs, long tail normally carried down, raised when the dog is excited. Short thick coat, smooth and glossy. Colors: fawn, blue, brindle, black or harlequin.

The Great Dane is probably crossbred from the English Mastiff and the Irish Wolfhound. The breed served as a boarhound in 19th century Germany when boars abounded and boar hunting was popular. Only the largest and

Collecting another award is Ch. Honey Hollow Miss Sepia, bred and trained by Lina Basquette Gilmore, Honey Hollow Kennels, Chalfont, Pennsylvania. Miss Sepia is not the only star of the picture—some readers may remember Mrs. Gilmore when she was a popular star in silent movies. They didn't give Oscars in those days, but the only prizes Mrs. Gilmore is interested in today are for her Great Danes.

bravest kind of dog was suitable for tackling such large and savage game. This magnificent animal is sheer poetry in motion, a study in power, coordination and rhythm. He eats a lot.

Mrs. Frederick W. Seward of Goshen, New York, is the owner of Ch. Loramo de la Colina.

GREAT PYRENEES

Size: Male, 27″ to 32″ high; female, 25″ to 29″ high; average length from shoulder blades to root of tail same as height. *Weight:* Male, 100 to 125 pounds; female, 90 to 115 pounds. *Standard:* Soundly built, heavily boned and of immense size, yet carries himself with great majesty, elegance and beauty. Chest deep, shoulders close to body, haunches rather prominent. Head large and wedge-shaped with rounded crown like a brown bear, and flat cheeks. Eyes slightly oblique, dark rich brown with close eyelids and well pigmented. Lips edged with black. Ears V-shaped but round-tipped, medium size, parallel with eyes, carried low and close to head except when raised at attention. Tail long enough to hang below hocks, well plumed, carried low when resting, and when alert, curls high over back "making the wheel." Coat protects against severe weather, with heavy fine white undercoat and long flat thick outer coat of coarser hair, straight or slightly wavy. Colors: all white or principally white with markings of badger, gray or varying shades of tan.

The Great Pyrenees has a noble history of service to mankind that goes back to the Bronze Age, but it was in the lonely mountain pastures of the Pyrenees that he gained his reputation as a devoted, intelligent, invaluable companion of the shepherd, equal in worth to two men. Nature endowed him with a long heavy coat to withstand not only the severest weather but attacks from roaming packs of wild animals and he was almost unbeatable in vanquishing wolves and bears so that he became known as the Pyrenean wolf dog or hound and Pyrenean bearhound.

Although General Lafayette presented a Great Pyrenees to his friend, Mr. J. S. Skinner, in 1824, it was not until 1933 that the actual breeding of the dog took place in America, but he has risen high in esteem and in number since. This beautiful animal is outstanding as a watchdog and companion but is eminently suited for sports as a guide and for pack work on ski trips. Serious in play and in work, the Great Pyrenees molds himself to the moods, desires, even the very life of his master, and is capable of great sacrifice. Gentle and docile, he is excellent with children.

GREYHOUND

Size: 26″ to 27″ high. *Weight:* Male, 65 to 70 pounds; female, 60 to 65 pounds. *Standard:* Tall, slender and streamlined in appearance with long arched back, deep chest and straight legs; low, well-bent hocks. Long, narrow head,

There is a quality of frozen motion in the true-to-type beauty of this superb female Greyhound, Ch. Jocelyn Blue, owned by Dr. Elsie S. Neustadt of Quincy, Massachusetts.

long, fine muzzle. Very long, arched neck; small ears thrown back; tail down and curved, long and slender. Coat is short, smooth and tight-fitting. Any color or marking.

Fleet as the wind, the epitome of grace in motion or still, the Greyhound has all the hauteur of a natural-born aristocrat among dogs. The Greyhound can trace his ancestry back to almost Biblical times, for he is depicted in the tombs of ancient Egyptian kings. In Egypt the nobility lavished such care and luxury on him that he was ardently hated by the oppressed populace.

He is a natural hunter of small game, but nowadays he is used most of all to chase a small mechanical rabbit around race tracks.

GRIFFON (Wire-haired Pointing)

Size: 19″ to 24″ high. *Weight:* 50 to 60 pounds. *Standard:* Like a pointer in build but more heavily cast; strong and vigorous. Short back, a trifle low on the leg. Head long and narrow, muzzle square, eyes large and not too dark, nose brown, moderate-sized ears hang flat. Tail docked, carried off the body. Coat shaggy, hard and stiff, rather rough, with downy undercoat. Bushy eyebrows and moustache. Colors: steel gray, gray-white, with chestnut-colored splashes, or chestnut.

First bred by a Hollander in 1870, the Wire-haired Pointing Griffon became popular throughout France and Germany as a rough sporting dog, skillful at retrieving on land or on water.

GRIFFON
Essayons d'Argent, owned by Mr. and Mrs. Chris Robertson of Wantagh, Long Island, N. Y.

In personality the Griffon has three strong traits: adaptability to his master, gentleness and humility. He responds to his master's desires, is eager to please, and is a versatile hunting dog. At home the Griffon has fine manners, meets strangers with proper reserve and raises a real rumpus only when he thinks his loved ones are in danger. Children recognize a Griffon's gentleness.

The Griffon seems to know that he's not pretty and not a mental giant. He is never smart-alecky nor a bully but humble in the love he gives his master and receives in turn.

IRISH SETTER

Size: 23" to 26" high. *Weight:* 50 to 60 pounds. *Standard:* Strong and deep-bodied but graceful. Lean, long head; low-set ears close to head; deep, square muzzle. Tail outstretched gracefully. Rather short but fine hair, longer on the ears, chest and underbody. Colors: mahogany red or golden chestnut; to show, must have no tracing of black.

This beautiful red dog from the Emerald Isle is a dashing, devil-may-care Irishman, bold, tough, but at the same time gentle, gay, lovable and loyal. He was brought over to this country for sporting purposes, and although his good

American and Canadian Champion, Laurel Ridge Star Rocket, Irish Setter winner of five shows, stands at attention for his owner, Mrs. Merritt M. Swartz of Laurel Ridge Kennels, Canton, Massachusetts.

looks and personality led his fanciers to breed him for show, he is still primarily a good hunting companion and high-class gun dog on all kinds of game. He can endure long workouts in the brush, is seldom stiff or sore and almost never ill-tempered when corrected. Although he frequently requires more training than some other breeds, once he's trained, it is for life and he need not be retrained each season. Every owner of an Irish Setter extols his virtues in appearance, personality and performance.

IRISH TERRIER

Size: About 18″ high. *Weight:* 25 to 27 pounds. *Standard:* Body fairly long, back arched, legs perfectly straight, muscular and strong. Tail high and dark. Head long and narrow with powerful jaws and teeth. Eyes dark, ears small, V-shaped and dropped forward. Coat thick and wiry in texture. Colors: red, wheaten, golden or bright red.

The Irish Terrier differs from other terriers in being slightly houndlike in outline, with a more decided trend to racing lines. He is almost a miniature of the Irish Wolfhound. Courageous and often a daredevil when faced with danger, he was used as a messenger dog in wartime.

This fine Irish Terrier is owned by breeder Rudolph Jensen of Chicago, Illinois.

CH. NUT BROWN SUSAN

An incomparable companion, he is loyal and protective of those he loves. He is equally at home in the country, city or camp, in the northland or the tropics. Always eager to join in fun and romp, he is a child's playmate and guardian.

Ch. Mahoney's O'Toole is the name of this friendly dog. The Irish Water Spaniel is well equipped for water.

IRISH WATER SPANIEL

Size: Male, 22" to 24" high; female, 21" to 23" high. *Weight:* Male, 55 to 65 pounds; female, 45 to 58 pounds. *Standard:* Smart, dashing and eager, strongly built but not leggy. Cleanly chiseled head, skull rather large, muzzle square and longish, deep mouth. Characteristic topknot of long loose curls growing down to well-defined peak between eyes. Eyes set flush, no eyebrows. Long lobular ears set low, abundantly covered with long curls. Body of medium length, long arching neck, high powerful hindquarters. Striking tail thick at root and covered for a few inches with short curls, tapering to a fine point with short smooth hairs, typical rat-tail in appearance. Coat of dense, tight, crisp ringlets, not woolly, shorter on front of legs. Colors: solid liver, no white on chest.

The tallest of the spaniels, the Irish Water Spaniel is the clown of the family because of his odd peaked topknot of curls and the quizzical expression of his eyes. He is at his best in the water, for his long curls tend to catch burrs on land. He is standoffish and forbidding to strangers, but loyal to those he knows.

IRISH WOLFHOUND

Size: 30″ to 34″ high. *Weight:* 105 to 140 pounds. *Standard:* A tall, powerful animal, swift and keen-sighted, with long back and arched loins. Long head and muzzle, slightly tapering. Small ears folded back along head. Long tail carried in low curve. Rough, wiry coat, bristling over eyes and along underjaw. Colors: gray, red, brindle, black, white and fawn.

The Irish Wolfhound is one of the old-timers in the history of dogdom. Hundreds of years before the Christian era these great galloping hounds with their piercing eyes and fierce eyebrows were brought to Greece by the attacking Celts. They were highly prized in early Roman days, and throughout the centuries that followed, for their prowess as hunters fit to hunt with kings. They are still hunters today, able to take and kill a wolf singlehanded, but more often they are valued pets, gentle and trustworthy despite their commanding appearance.

Docile as a lamb is this Irish Wolfhound, Ch. Victoria of Killybracken, owned by Mrs. C. Groverman Ellis and Miss Mary Jane Ellis, Killybracken Kennels, Wayne, Illinois.

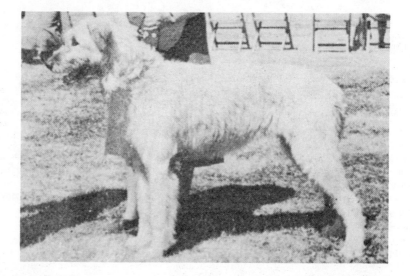

Blue Heather of Geddesburg, one of the fine specimens of Italian Greyhounds which are owned and handled by Anne W. Korotnev of New York City.

ITALIAN GREYHOUND

Size: About 10″ high. *Weight:* 6 to 10 pounds (2 classes: under 8 pounds and over 8 pounds). *Standard:* A Greyhound in miniature, with long, gracefully arched neck and shoulders, deep narrow chest, and curved back that droops at the hindquarters. Straight legs have small delicate bones with long hare-like feet. Long, flat and narrow skull with very fine muzzle, dark nose, and rather large bright eyes full of expression. Ears rose shaped, soft, delicate and placed well back. Thin satiny coat. Fairly long tail carried low Colors: all shades of fawn, red, mouse, blue, cream and white.

The elegant Italian Greyhound has a glorious heritage as the favorite of royalty and privileged classes, not for any use but simply because of his marvelous disposition and small size. His history goes back to the days of ancient Pompeii and for many centuries he was the only known pet dog of Italian nobility. In fact, "beware of the dog" mottos uncovered in old Roman villas meant that guests should watch their steps so as not to hurt the owner's tiny Italian Greyhound, which could easily be crushed by a careless step—quite a switch from the meaning of our present-day "beware of dog" signs! He existed in his present form for more than 2000 years although he underwent considerable refinement in England and Scotland, particularly during the late-Victorian period.

Many interesting stories are told about the Italian Greyhound. One concerns Frederick the Great, King of Prussia, who carried his favorite Italian Greyhound wherever he went. Once during the Seven Years' War, he was in a precarious position and had to take refuge, dog in arms, under a bridge, over which the Austrian dragoons were passing. The dog clung to his master and by not uttering a sound saved the king from capture. When this dog died, Frederick buried him with his own hands in the palace grounds.

Although he has the grace and high-stepping pace of the Greyhound, the Italian Greyhound is solely a pet, noted for his loyalty and charm, cleanliness and ease in training. There is increasing interest in this rare breed in America.

JAPANESE SPANIEL

Size: About 9" high but size varies, the smaller the better. *Weight:* About 7 pounds. *Standard:* Square, compact body, wide in chest, "cobby" in shape, length equalling height. Head rather large for dog's size, with broad skull, rounded in front, very short muzzle. Nose the color of dog's markings (i.e.,

Outstanding winner Ch. Budah's Mr. Kido won 33 Best of Breed awards at the age of 2 years. He was home-bred by owner Mrs. Dora B. Wadsworth, Budorah House of Champions, Denver, Colorado.

black in black-marked dog, red or deep flesh in red- or lemon-marked dog). Large, dark, lustrous eyes, rather prominent and set wide apart. Small V-shaped feathered ears set wide apart, high on head and carried slightly forward. Profuse, straight but long coat, thick ruff around neck, feathered thighs and tail. Profusely-feathered tail is well twisted to either right or left from root and carried up over back, flowing on opposite side. Colors: black and white or red and white (red includes all shades of sable, brindle, lemon and orange).

Old Chinese temples, pottery and embroideries picture dogs closely resembling the Japanese Spaniel or Japanese Chin. This adds weight to the speculation that the toy breed is very old, originating in China centuries ago. It is believed that one of the Chinese emperors gave a pair to the emperor of Japan. The dogs were kept by royalty and often used as gifts of esteem to diplomats and foreigners. Commodore Perry was one who received these dogs and he in turn presented a pair to Queen Victoria. In time these specimens came to America. During World War II, the supply was severely curtailed so the breed could be maintained and improved only with what was on hand.

Oriental in appearance, the Japanese Spaniel looks aristocratic and high-bred, dainty and well-mannered. He moves stylishly, lifting his feet high and carrying his heavily feathered tail proudly curved. He is lively and alert and wonderful around children. Naturally clean and game, he thrives in almost any climate and makes an ideal pet. As a rule, he is a regular ham in the show ring, and clowns around the house, although he's not rough or noisy. The Japanese Spaniel is sensitive, though, with definite likes and dislikes, but he is ever faithful to his master.

KEESHOND

Size: 17" to 18" high. *Weight:* 35 to 45 pounds. *Standard:* Body cobby and well ribbed. Tail placed high and carried in a tight curl over the back. Plume and skirts pale cream in color as are legs and feet. Face very distinctive; dark muzzle, alert almond eyes and small ivy-shaped ears present a "what-is-it?" expression. Spectacles (dark pencillings running from corners of eyes out toward the ears) very noticeable in the best specimens. Coat full with long straight hair. Colors: gray and black, the outer layer black-tipped, the under layer pale gray or cream.

The Keeshond, descended from an Arctic breed, is the national dog of Holland. Formerly he guarded slow-moving canal barges and was named for Kees de Gyselaer, a patriot of Holland in the 18th century. Unbothered by extremes in temperature, the Keeshond is easily kept. His coat sheds dirt and is highly resistant to parasites or disease as well as acting as insulation against heat or cold.

He often serves as a child's pet, family watchdog and companion because of his affectionate nature and attractive appearance. Living in the bosom of Dutch families, caring for the children, sharing the home life, the Keeshond

desires companionship and approval, has no false dignity, learns tricks and obedience routines easily and remembers them.

Because they have "cast-iron" stomachs, they make delightful car and boat companions. The Keeshond can smile, baring his teeth in an ingratiating grin. He is sometimes known as The Smiling Dutchman.

KERRY BLUE TERRIER

Size: 17½″ to 19½″ high. *Weight:* 33 to 40 pounds. *Standard:* Well-knit, well-balanced and well-developed muscular body on straight staunch legs. Short, strong and level back, well-sprung ribs, and muscular hindquarters free from droop or crouch. Powerful jaws covered with whiskers; small dark eyes, especially keen and expressive; V-shaped ears dropped forward close to cheeks with top of folded ear slightly above level of skull. Docked tail set on high, the straighter the better, carried gaily. Soft, thick, wavy coat unlike usual wiry terrier coat. Colors: deep slate to light blue-gray. (Puppies usually born black but develop blue color by about a year.)

From the mountainous regions of County Kerry, the Kerry Blue Terrier rose to be national dog of the Irish Republic. He was used for hunting small game and birds, for retrieving from land and water and even for herding sheep and cattle, but quickly gained favor as a bench show dog. Gentle, lovable and intelligent, the Kerry still retains his trailing and retrieving powers and in addition is a superb watchdog and companion, able to put up a good plucky fight with his foes. He is easy to train and is long-lived—Kerries at 6 and 8 years of age are considered young dogs!

KERRY BLUE
Ch. Kerrimac As You Like It, a champion at 15 months and a top stud dog. Owner is
James W. McBurney of Kerrimac Kennels, Wadsworth, Illinois.

KUVASZ

Size: Male about 26" high; female somewhat less. *Weight:* 80 pounds and more (up to 150 pounds). *Standard:* Sturdily built, body well-ribbed, chest broad and deep. Muscular. Head rather long, covered with short fine hair. Muzzle clean-cut, rather square. Ears high set, medium V-shaped, slightly offset from the skull. Tail of moderate length, set deep, tip slightly turned up. Coat long and wavy. Color: white.

The giant Kuvasz probably comes from Tibet via Russia but was first bred in Hungary by King Matthias I who reigned from 1458 to 1490. This king trusted no one and decided to breed these dogs for his own protection. The royal family kept the breed secret until long afterward. Finally they were allowed to be employed as sheep dogs and were very useful at that chore as they are reliable, hard-working and responsible guardians. They quickly learn the boundaries of their property and never stray from it. Kuvaszok (the plural) have also been used for hunting big game and bear and as seeing-eye dogs.

It's amazing to find this huge animal so very gentle, well behaved and placid with extreme love for children. He is odorless and only barks when necessary.

Ch. Condor Oznerol, belonging to Mr. and Mrs. Nicholas De Lorenzo of Oznerol Kennels, Peakville, New York.

This fine Labrador is owned by David D. Elliot, Lloyd Harbor, Long Island, N. Y.

LABRADOR RETRIEVER

Size: Male, 22½" to 24½" high; female, 21½" to 23½" high. *Weight:* Male, 60 to 75 pounds; female, 55 to 70 pounds. *Standard:* Wide skull, slight stop, clean-cut and free from fleshy cheeks; long powerful jaws, not snipey, wide, well-developed nostrils; ears rather far back, hang moderately loosely, not large or heavy. Powerful neck and long, sloping shoulders, straight, somewhat short legs. Distinctive tail very thick toward base, gradually tapering, free from feathering but densely furred and rounded and otter-like in appearance; may be gaily carried but not curled over back. Short, very dense coat, straight and fairly hard to the touch. Color: generally black; other whole colors permissible.

The close, dense coat of the Labrador Retriever enables the dog to enter the iciest of waters without wetting his skin, and its shortness prevents tangling and the formation of ice on the fur. His sense of smell is incredibly keen and he is extremely rapid both running and swimming. The Labrador Retriever actually originated in Newfoundland, and it is not known how he reached Labrador.

A fine specimen of this trim and jaunty breed is Ch. Tully Token owned by Mrs. Louis Loeb, Woodrise Kennels, Greenwich, Connecticut.

LAKELAND TERRIER

Size: Not more than 15" high. *Weight:* Male, not over 17 pounds; female, not over 16 pounds. *Standard:* Moderately broad skull and broad, strong muzzle. Ears fall forward. Harsh, wiry coat in several shades of tan, brown, red, wheaten, blue or black. Tail docked, not too short, and gaily carried.

A trim, small but workmanlike dog requiring no pampering, the Lakeland Terrier was bred originally to do a hard day's work killing fox and otter of the rugged Lakeland country. The pet of today has inherited the jaunty spirit and physical toughness of his ancestors and is extremely clean in his habits. His wiry coat is weather- and dirt-resistant, presents no shedding problem and requires a minimum of care and trimming in order to maintain its smart appearance. The Lakeland Terrier has a keen sense of fun and a real family spirit—he will join happily in a romp with the children as well as a quiet snooze before the fire.

LHASA APSO

Size: 10" to 11" high, 14" to 15" long. *Weight:* About 15 to 16 pounds.
Standard: Body covered with long straight heavy coat that falls down over eyes
and forms whiskers and beard. Short muscular legs covered with hair right
down to and including round feet. Head narrow, muzzle fairly short, eyes dark.
Ears hanging and fringed, tail feathered. Colors: parti-color, lion-like colors
preferred. Also golden, black, white, brown, slate or smoke. Many colors occur
in each litter.

The little Lhasa Apso which comes from the sacred city of Lhasa in Tibet
was a watchdog in the homes of the lamas (priests) 800 years ago. The gay
and lively Lhasa Apso is deeply devoted to his family, highly intelligent and

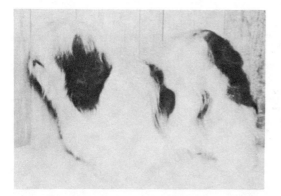

Left: Ming Fu-Tzu was
bred by Eloris and L. R.
Liebmann of Miradel Kennels in Los Gatos, California. The owner is Georgia
Palmer of Annison, Illinois.

Below: These 2½-month-old pups were champion
sired. Their dame was a
show winner, bred by the
Liebmanns too.

easily trained. He may not readily accept a stranger, holding himself aloof, but is not timid or shy. He returns kindness with a desire to please and is becoming more and more popular as a pet.

MALTESE

Size: About 5" high. *Weight:* 2 to 7 pounds. *Standard:* Short small body covered by straight silky coat hanging down low on either side, parted down the back from nose to tail. No undercoat. Fairly long muzzle with big black nostrils, and dark eyes, preferably black-rimmed. Ears feathered and dropped. Tail curls over the back. Color: white.

A paradoxical little animal, the Maltese is even smaller than he looks! Tiny enough to be carried about in one's sleeve, he was the favorite pet and plaything of aristocratic women of ancient Greece and Rome. His long silky white coat and feathers obviously require a lot of attention—on however small a scale—but the result is rewarding.

MALTESE
Every inch a champion, and doesn't she know it! Ch. Electa Caroline of Oak Manor at 3½ pounds is a small compact female of superb quality, an Italian import. She is owned by Mrs. W. Burg of Oak Manor Kennels, Lumberville, Pennsylvania.

MANCHESTER TERRIER (Standard and Toy)

Size: Standard, about 16" high; Toy, about 7" high. *Weight:* Standard, 12 to 22 pounds; Toy, 5 to 12 pounds. *Standard:* Except for size and ear carriage, the Standard and Toy are remarkably alike with sleek, streamlined body, narrow chest, short back and arched loin. Narrow, wedge-shaped heads, extremely tight-lipped jaws and small sparkling oblong-shaped eyes. Thin ears close together at the top of head; the Standard has semi-erect ears unless cropped when they point straight up; the Toy has naturally erect ears. Moderately short

Toy Manchester Terrier Ch. Bam Saw's Bummet Brook Brandy, is a born "ham" and loves shows, according to his owners, Mr. L. S. Worthen and Mrs. Samuel L. Hobbs of Bummet Brook Farm, Shrewsbury, Massachusetts. He finished his championship with 3 majors by the age of 13 months and had 3 Group placings before he was 18 months. He is a proven stud besides being a "wonderful house dog, getting along with all ages — four-legged and two-legged."

tail, thick at base, tapering to a fine point, carried no higher than the back. Close short coat, glossy but not soft. Colors: black and tan (rich mahogany tan).

Once a poor man's rat-killing and rabbit-coursing dog in the Manchester district of England, the Manchester Terrier of today with his sleek svelte appearance (inherited from his Whippet strain) is a far cry from his rough-and-tumble vermin dog ancestors. However, he still has the old fight in him and will tackle anything up to twice his size and gamely hold his own. He is intelligent, a staunch friend and watchdog who misses nothing both in sight and action. Town dwellers particularly enjoy him as a house dog because of his cleanliness and lack of odor. His short black hair also does not shed easily or cling to a garment or furniture. He's equally at home in the country where his wide-awake terrier instincts stand him in good stead.

The Toy Manchester Terrier is no longer a separate breed but a variety, according to his present-day fanciers who are rapidly increasing in number. The development of the Toy was a matter of chance at first. Occasionally two standard specimens produced a litter which included one that was considerably smaller than the others. These small puppies attracted so much attention that breeders tried to produce more of the same size and for a while there resulted a great many unscrupulous practices among breeders who tried to supply the demand. At one time the Toy weight was reduced to around 2½ pounds but these tiny mites did not survive for long and hence became less popular. The Toy has the same characteristics as his larger relative in pluck, friendliness, alert watchfulness and cleanliness and is highly prized by his owners.

Above: Mooreleigh Maurice and Mooreleigh Michael are father and son. Left: Mooreleigh Michael lies in watchful repose. The owner is Marie Moore, Mooreleigh Kennels, The Plains, Virginia.

MASTIFF

Size: 27½" to 33" high. *Weight:* 165 to 185 pounds. *Standard:* A massive dog, broad, muscular and powerful. Head broad, muzzle blunt and squarish. Small ears lying close to cheeks in repose, forehead markedly wrinkled, eyes small and wide-set. Dense short coat, close-lying. Colors: apricot, silver fawn or dark fawn brindle, with ears, nose and muzzle dark, the blacker the better.

Mastiffs have a continuous history from the most ancient times right up to the present. Marco Polo wrote that when he visited the Kublai Khan he found 5000 Mastiffs kept for the purpose of hunting lions and other big game! In England during Anglo-Saxon times, the law required that large estates keep Mastiffs as guards. Some say that Mastiffs first came to America on the Mayflower, and others say they were imported later to guard property. The fearsome enemy of wild animals and harmful foes, he is very gentle with children and even with small domestic animals, and he will disdainfully push aside with his paw a terrier who has nipped at him!

82

MINIATURE PINSCHER

Size: 10″ to 12½″ high. *Weight:* 6 to 10 pounds. *Standard:* A toy-sized terrier, intelligent, alert, active. Compact, with furious, lively manner. Flat head tapers toward muzzle. Smooth-coated, naturally well-groomed. Eyes dark and bright. Ears erect when cropped. Tail docked. Short, shining coat. Precise, hackneyed gait. Colors: black, with reddish-rust markings; red; brown with yellow or rust markings.

Although similar to the Doberman but on a smaller scale, the Miniature Pinscher has a nature and a way suggestive of a larger dog. He is especially valuable as a watchdog, sometimes keener than a dog twice his size. He is a born show dog and often used on the stage. His coat requires scant attention. The "Minpin" has a fondness for home and master that is exceptional. Existing for several centuries in Germany, he has been bred in the Scandinavian countries, elsewhere in Europe and more recently in the United States since 1929.

This champion Miniature Pinscher is owned by Hertha von der Kammer-Brugger, Cinderella Kennels, The Bronx, New York.

Ch. Little Bear's Roaring Main owned by Margaret Booth Chern of Little Bear Kennels, New Milford, Connecticut, winner of the Best of Breed in Working Dog Group at Westminster, 1958-1959.

NEWFOUNDLAND

Size: 20″ to 28″ high. *Weight:* 110 to 150 pounds. *Standard:* A strong dog with a slight rolling gait. Broad, massive head. Muzzle short, clean-cut and square. Coat flat and dense. If brushed the wrong way, it should fall back into place naturally. Bones massive throughout. Tail moderate length. Color: dull jet black; symmetry desirable.

Domesticated by the American Indian and a close member of the Indian family, the Newfoundland would dive for fish, retrieve game, pull heavy loads, guard and play games with the children. He holds an unsurpassed record for saving lives in stormy seas.

His benevolence, strength and intelligence captured the imagination of early American settlers and the dog became part of many a ship's crew, ready to give a hand with a line or rescue a man overboard. Exported to every foreign country, the breed fetched fabulous prices.

In Barrie's *Peter Pan,* Nana, the nursemaid, was a Newfoundland. Wagner called the breed Nature's own gentleman. The Newfoundland today is a perfect family dog.

NORWEGIAN ELKHOUND
Above: Ch. Trygvie Vik-
ingsson of Craftsdal Ken-
nels was bred and handled
by Mrs. Glenna C. Crafts
of Cuyahoga Falls, Ohio.
Right: This is a 35-day-
old Norwegian Elkhound
puppy on his first day
outdoors.

NORWEGIAN ELKHOUND

Size: 18" to 20½" high. *Weight:* About 50 pounds. *Standard:* Medium size, powerful, compact, short body. Head broad at ears, no loose skin. High, firm, erect *prick* ears, pointed and mobile. Thick, rich coat, rather smooth; soft, woolly undercoat. Short tail set high, thick close hair tightly curled but no brush. Color: gray with black-tipped hairs.

Comrade to the Vikings, the Norwegian Elkhound's history goes back more than 6000 years. The Elkhound is unusual in that his distinctive type was achieved by natural methods. No form was imposed on him; he was not squeezed into a preconceived standard. His structure and rare beauty were evolved from tests of performance. The dog was mainly used in the hunting of elk (known in the United States as moose).

The Elkhound has highly developed senses and can scent a body at two and three miles. In attacking an elk, the dog bounces like a rubber ball, jumps nimbly in and out, giving full tongue to his high-pitched voice.

Not a show dog until 1877, he has recently been exported in ever increasing numbers. As a pet he is friendly and dependable. He was too gentle and kindly to be taught to attack people for the canine corps. He requires no clipping nor bathing and is easily groomed and trained.

(See photos on previous page.)

NORWICH TERRIER

Size: 9" to 11" high (ideal, 10"). *Weight:* 10 to 14 pounds (ideal, 11 pounds). *Standard:* Compact, moderately short body with well-sprung ribs, level back, strong, rounded and powerful hindquarters and short, strong neck on clean shoulders. Short but powerful straight legs, thickly padded round feet. Wide, slightly rounded skull with strong, "foxy" muzzle, tight-lipped clean jaws and scissors bite. Eyes are expressive, bright and dark. Small neat ears set wide apart, prick or drop. Medium-docked tail. Hard, straight, wiry coat lies close to body with definite undercoat. Except for slight eyebrows and whiskers, hair on head, ears and muzzle short and smooth. Colors: red, red-wheaten, black and tan or grizzle.

Some people think the Norwich Terrier should be called the Cantab Terrier in honor of the Cambridge University students who made him a fad around the 1880's. He was called the Jones Terrier then, after a foremost English breeder, and brought to the United States after World War I as a hunt dog. Despite his short legs, he has no trouble keeping up with horses, and is tremendously active and rugged, able to withstand all kinds of weather. For all his demon qualities, the Norwich Terrier has a lovable disposition and makes an ideal house dog as his hard, close coat does not collect dirt and needs no trimming. He's a one-man dog and once he pledges his loyalty, it's for life.

Ch. Tuff was voted the Standard of Perfection for Norwich Terriers and is sire of outstanding winners. Tuff belongs to Miss Sylvia Warren of Dover, Massachusetts.

OLD ENGLISH SHEEPDOG

Size: 21″ to 25″ high. *Weight:* 50 to 65 pounds. *Standard:* Strong, compact body of great symmetry, measuring practically the same from shoulder to stern as in height, and free from legginess. Ribs well sprung; brisket deep, capacious. Stout, slightly arched loins and round, muscular hindquarters with densely coated hams. Forelegs dead straight, galloping with great elasticity, walking or trotting with characteristic amble. Rather square-shaped skull well covered with hair; jaw fairly long, strong, square and truncated. Color of eyes varies but usually dark, and in blue dogs, a pearl, walleye or china eye is typical. Medium-sized ears lie flat to side of head. Profuse but not excessive coat is hard, shaggy and free from curl. Naturally tailless, or tail docked so short when puppy is whelped that he's nicknamed "bobtail." Colors: any shade of gray, grizzle, blue or blue-merle with or without white markings or in reverse.

Despite his name, the Old English Sheepdog is not so old in origin, and the earliest picture depicting the present-day specimen is a painting by Gainsborough in which the Duke of Buccleuch (1771) has his arms clasped about

OLD ENGLISH SHEEPDOG

Ch. Fezziwig Ceiling Zero proudly displays his No. 1 championship status. He is owned by Mr. H. B. Van Rensselaer of Fezziwig Kennels, Summit, New Jersey.

the neck of what appears to be an Old English Sheepdog. He was a tax-exempt "drover's dog," used largely for driving sheep and cattle into the city markets, and his bobbed tail was a sign of his working status—hence, some believe, his affectionate nickname of "bob" and "bobtail."

He is home-loving, not given to roaming and fighting, and is extremely agile, with an affinity for water and a "soft" or tender mouth so that he can be easily trained to retrieve. His intelligence, sympathetic understanding and capacity for love (which is as big as his capacious body), and lack of boisterousness combine to make him an ideal house dog, equally at home in an apartment or large house. His coat helps him adapt to any climatic conditions and acts as an insulation against heat, cold and dampness, and actually requires no greater care than any other long-haired dog. Regular grooming with a stiff brush is ample, and if his coat becomes matted, tangles can be separated easily with the·fingers. He is a fine companion for children and is so amiable and tractable that no owner can speak highly enough about him as a pet.

PAPILLON

Size and Weight: No more than 11" high at withers, weight in proportion. *Standard:* Head appears small, skull slightly rounded, well-defined stop, fine tapering muzzle, black nose flat on top. Eyes dark and round, but not bulging. Coat fine and silky, no undercoat, abundant chest and collar, ears and back of forelegs fringed, tail plumed and arched over back and to one side. Ears most distinctive feature: large and plentifully fringed, carried obliquely erect like wings of butterfly. Colors: any pure solid color, tricolored or bicolored.

This toy dog was named Papillon by the French because his beautiful widespread ears resemble the butterfly. A drop-eared dog, identical with the Papillon in every other respect, is popular on the Continent, where he is known as the Phalene. In America Papillons are bred for erect ears, although the drop type is recognized and judged equally.

PAPILLON
A proud little handful is Ch. Avis of Autumn Acres. Her sire and dame, both imported from Belgium, were Ch. Bellor and Ch. Zelie du Petite Paon. Her owner is Mrs. Lottie D. Armour of Oldwick, New Jersey.

Male and female Pekes make equally good pets.

PEKINGESE

Size: 6″ to 9″ high. *Weight:* Usually 6 to 10 pounds, always under 14 pounds. *Standard:* Massive, wide, broad, flat skull, wide between large, dark, prominent eyes. Chinese expression. Heavy overcoat over long, thick, silk, straight coat; a profuse ruff on the shoulders, neck, forechest; luxuriant fringes on heart-shaped ears, legs, underbody and tail. Tail set high, heavily plumed, carried to one side over back. Colors: all, especially red, fawn, black, black and tan, sable, brindle, white and parti-color; black masks and spectacles around eyes, with lines to ears.

The happy little toy dog we know as the Pekingese was once known as the little Lion Dog of Peking; in those days, however, he was much larger. The Emperor's dogs lived in the sacred temple and the puppies were often nursed by slave girls. Theft of one of the royal dogs was punishable by death, as the Pekingese was one of the sacred symbols of China.

The "Peke" was first introduced to the Western world in 1860 when the British broke into the Imperial Palace. One of the dogs was brought to England and given to Queen Victoria, who named it Looty in honor of the lieutenant whose gift it was. Near the end of the 19th century, a dowager princess in China became friendly with Americans and gave gifts to Alice Roosevelt, J. P. Morgan and others. However, most of the breeding stock came to America from England.

The Pekingese is a lot of dog in a small package. In public he carries himself in a haughty, dignified manner. At home he drops his airs and relishes a rollicking romp. A fine watchdog for his size, the Peke is not at all delicate. He thrives in either hot or cold climate.

POINTER

Size: 24" to 25" high. *Weight:* Male, 50 to 55 pounds; female, 45 to 50 pounds. *Standard:* Long skull, well-developed occipital ridge, furrow between eyes; long muzzle, wide-open nostrils; soft, medium-sized ears lying close to cheeks, set on low, no tendency to prick or fold. Strong back rising slightly to long shoulders, wide hips, long tail carried above line of back without curl. Legs rather short, bony, straight and strong. Short, flat, firm coat. Colors: white with spots of liver, brown, black, lemon or orange.

Anyone who has ever seen a Pointer "on a bird" knows how he got his name: his whole taut body, from the tail to the tip of his pointing nose, aims unerringly and steadfastly at the target, waiting for the gun. This superlative field trial dog with his lithe and nervous energy is an ideal choice for the hunter desirous of results. He is born to the hunt, and puppies as young as 2 months often point. He is a neat, clean dog, quick to learn and anxious to please by proper performance.

The prize Pointers in the field are owned and trained by George James Stymiest, Lambert-ville, New Jersey.

This German Shorthaired Pointer is graciously accepting a blue ribbon. She is owned by Mrs. Jean Paul Steele of Plaster City, California, was bred by Mr. M. E. Lamb, and her name is Ch. Paglo's Cindy.

Rusty V. Bergseithafen on the point. This fine specimen of German Wirehaired Pointer was raised by K. W. Mueller of Mueller's Retriever Kennels, Manitowoc, Wisconsin, and sold to Clark Gable in 1957.

POINTER (German Shorthaired)

Size: 21" to 25" high. *Weight:* 45 to 70 pounds. *Standard:* Heavy and powerful body but well balanced and clean-cut. Medium broad head with muzzle about same length as skull. Ears hang flat to head. Docked tail. Short, thick and tough coat. Colors: solid liver, liver and white spotted, ticked or roaned.

It would be hard to find a hunting dog of greater versatility than the German Shorthaired Pointer, a truly all-purpose dog. He is a keen bird dog who works equally well with duck, pheasant, quail, grouse, partridge, woodcock, rabbit, coon and opossum. He also trails and points deer. As a retriever he braves icy waters (thanks to his water-repellent coat and webbed feet) or any terrain when he is properly broken.

Selective breeding has aided in the pleasing conformation of this attractive dog, and also in his powers of endurance, which are exceptional. Besides being a hunting dog, he makes an excellent family watchdog and a fine companion.

POINTER (German Wirehaired)

Size: 21" to 25" high. *Weight:* 45 to 70 pounds. *Standard:* Big, clean-cut, powerful and muscular with short, straight back, broad hips and strong thighs. Moderately broad head, full lips that do not hang heavily, ears hanging flat to the head. Docked tail. Short coat is thick, tough and wiry. Colors: solid liver or liver and white-spotted, ticked or roaned.

Formerly known as a Deutscher Drahthaar, this splendid hunting dog owes his pointing skill to his Spanish forebears and his trailing skill to his Bloodhound ancestors. His wiry coat sheds water, making him a fine water dog, and on land he hunts close to the gun; no cover is too dense for him. He is staunch on the point, an excellent retriever on land or water, a good all-round hunter and a warm companion.

This picture shows how playful the Pomeranian can get. He is owned by Mrs. Georgie M. Sheppard of Basking Ridge, New Jersey.

POMERANIAN

Size: About 7″ high. *Weight:* 3 to 7 pounds. *Standard:* Body short and compact. Legs fine in bone and heavily feathered. Exhibits intelligence of expression, docility in disposition and buoyancy in deportment. Foxy head, small ears carried erect. Eyes slanting. Plumed tail lies flat over back. Coat thick and particularly heavy around the neck and chest where it forms a mane and frill. Colors: black, brown, chocolate-red, orange-cream, orange-sable, wolf-sable, beaver-blue, white and parti-color.

The perky little Pomeranian is really a sled dog in miniature. He has a double coat just as a Huskie and Samoyed does. He gets his name from the German province of Pomerania. It was there the breeders realized what a delightful house pet the "Pom" would make and bred the sheep-herding Pomeranian, which weighed as much as 30 pounds, down to toy size. From Germany the dogs were brought to England where they soon became popular. In America the breed has been shown since 1900.

The Pom is a delightful and active pet—playful, intelligent, courageous and loyal. Even an adult Pom seldom resists the pleasure of playing with toys. He gets along well with other pets in the household, even eating out of the same dish as the family cat. He will put on a great show of wanting to tangle with the largest dogs in the neighborhood.

94

POODLE (Standard, Miniature, and Toy)

Size: Standard, over 15" high; Miniature, 10 to 15" high; Toy, under 10" high. *Weight:* Standard, 45 to 55 pounds; Miniature, about 16 pounds; Toy, about 7 pounds. *Characteristics:* Three varieties of Poodle breed—Standard, Miniature, and Toy, but all identical, except for size. Built squarely with short and strong back. Flat cheeks, long finely-chiseled muzzle, oval and dark eyes and ears hanging close to the head. Tail docked and carried gaily. Heavy harsh coat may be curly or frizzy. Colors: black, brown, white, apricot, blue and silver solid colors.

Although Poodles make fine outdoor dogs, style of appearance is perhaps the most important characteristic of all three sizes. Several styles of clipping are sanctioned by tradition and do much to enhance the naturally graceful appearance of the dog, as well as to add to his comfort. And, since this dog makes an ideal pet, the clipping increases his acceptability within the household, since it prevents him from tracking mud indoors.

In all three sizes, Poodles make lively and intelligent pets, naturally hardy

Ch. Puttencove Promise, a Standard Poodle, was Best in Show in 1958 at the Westminster Kennels. He is owned by Mrs. George Putnam of Manchester, Massachusetts.

and easy to rear. Dignified though they may be in appearance, chic, stylish, even sporting a rhinestone collar, to their owners they are much like a child of the family, made to be pampered and fussed over by everyone.

PUG
International Ch. Picnic
Valley Sugar N' Spice
owned by Picnic Valley
Kennels of Novato, California. She is the dam of
three champions and the
holder of 19 Best of Breed
awards. This photo was
taken when she was 8
months old, before she
became a champion at the
early age of 10 months.

PUG

Size: 10″ to 11″ high. *Weight:* 14 to 18 pounds. *Standard:* Toy size with a wrinkled face, short back and round rib, rather low on his legs. The Pug head is massive for a dog so small. His muzzle is broad, square and very short. Eyes large and worried-looking. Ears are velvety and hang down. Tail tightly curled. Glossy coat short. Colors: black, silver or apricot with black face and black mark running down the back.

Chinese in origin, the Pug left the Orient many centuries ago for Holland and England and finally came to America. Wherever he goes, he becomes the most popular pet for a time. A favorite in small homes because of his toy size, the Pug is well-behaved and requires little care.

Ch. Gooseberry Hill Bandmaster won champion awards at 11 months and is the newest Puli champion in America. He is owned by Mr. and Mrs. John B. McManus of Gooseberry Hill Kennels, Oregon, Wisconsin.

PULI

Size: 17″ high, females slightly smaller. *Weight:* 30 to 35 pounds. *Standard:* Straight, long, muscular body; medium length muzzle; medium-large V-shaped ears carried flat to the side of head; close, deep-set eyes; fairly broad chest; medium tail carried low with end curling up but occasionally natural bobtail;

strong, straight, muscular forelegs; long profuse coat of wavy or curly fine hair, tumbles down head and face. Colors: solid black, shades of gray, or white.

Alert, courageous, intelligent and extremely active, the Puli (plural, Pulik) makes an ideal guard, companion and watchdog. He is versatile and easily trained and is excellent at herding sheep. His dazzling footwork also enables him to excel at rabbit hunting and retrieving water fowl. The Puli tends to be a one-man dog, and is unfriendly to strangers. He's a comparative newcomer to American dogdom, but thanks to his enthusiastic fanciers he is becoming increasingly popular.

RETRIEVER (Curly-Coated and Flat-Coated)

(Both varieties) *Size:* About 22" to 23" high. *Weight:* 60 to 70 pounds. *Standard:* (Curly) Short body, deep chest, back moderately long, tail carried straight out, curl-covered ears. Body a mass of curls to the tip of his tail. (Flat) Short-backed, squarely built, muscular. Legs straight, well boned, feathered. Neck clean, chest deep. Ears small. Tail feathered and long. Coat dense, fine and flat. Colors (both): black or liver.

The Curly-Coated Retriever is a descendant of the English Water Spaniel, and is distinguished by his curly-coated body. The tight curls shed the water and protect his skin from heavy brush.

The Flat-Coated Retriever is a combination of St. John's Newfoundland and Labrador Retriever, with later crosses with Golden Retriever and Setter. This type was developed in England of American parentage. Both Retrievers are active hunting dogs, at home in the water. The breed works well in field trials.

Rab of Morinda, a Flat-Coated Retriever, has won consistently in field trials for 10 years. He is owned by Dorothy W. Moroff of Aroma Park, Illinois.

The owner of this Rhodesian Ridgeback, William Howard O'Brien of Redhouse Kennels, Scottsdale, Arizona, was founder and president of the Rhodesian Ridgeback Club of America.

RHODESIAN RIDGEBACK

Size: Male, 25" to 27" high; female, 1" shorter. *Weight:* Male, 75 pounds; female, 65 pounds. *Standard:* Outstanding peculiarity is a distinct ridge down the back with hair growing in opposite direction to rest of coat. Strong, muscular, active, capable of great endurance with fair amount of speed. Hound type, head fairly long and broad. Muzzle long and deep. Body deep-chested. Legs straight. Tail long. Coat short and sleek. Colors: light wheaten to red wheaten.

Sometimes known as the African Lion Hound, the Rhodesian Ridgeback is a native of South Africa where he was bred by Boer farmers as a serviceable hunting dog. Fairly new as an A.K.C. recognized breed, he's an all-around hunter. He has a keen sense of smell and sight, is alert, takes orders well and is capable of speed up to 35 miles per hour. His webbed feet make him an excellent swimmer. He does not bark without provocation but has been known to hold an intruder at bay for hours.

No matter how much he is pulled, pummelled or ridden, the Ridgeback is friendly with children and interested in them.

Ch. Stan von Reichboden finished his championship at Valley Forge in 1956 in a record entry for the Best of 14 Rottweilers. He was bred and handled by his owners, Mr. and Mrs. J. D. Bean of Reichboden Kennels, Greenfield, Ohio.

ROTTWEILER

Size: 21¾" to 27" high. *Weight:* 80 to 90 pounds. *Standard:* Built stockily, rather heavily boned, with short, broad, straight back; broad chest, muscular thighs, straight legs. Head broad with muzzle about as long as depth of skull. Good-humored expression in small eyes. Ears are high-set and hang flat. Short coat is very thick and hard. Tail short, docked if necessary. Color: black with tan markings.

The Rottweiler is a lesson in the history of Western civilization. When the ancient Romans set about conquering the world one of their problems was the supply of fresh food for their armies. Since beef travelled on the hoof, many dogs were needed to help drive the cattle across the Alps and into the lands beyond. As the cattle were slaughtered and eaten, the dogs were no longer needed, so the Romans left them behind wherever they happened to be. There were several breeds used by the Romans, and the ancestors of the present-day Rottweilers stayed with the diminishing herds much longer than most. They ended up in Rottweil, in the center of livestock country, and there for many centuries they were bred as working dogs indispensable to butchers and cattle merchants. Tough and hardy dogs were needed, for above and beyond the rigors of cattle herding was the danger of marauding cattle thieves and also thieves who were after gold. It is told that merchants on their way to buy cattle would tie their bags of money to the dogs' necks, knowing that no thief would be fool-hardy enough to attempt going after the tough Rottweiler.

When cattle was shipped by rail instead of being driven, the breed of dogs almost died out, but early in this century the breed was revived when it was found to have the intelligence and hardiness necessary for police work. The Rottweiler has developed more character through police work, and he possesses those characteristics of loyalty, affection for his "family" and self-reliance which make him an excellent choice as a pet.

ST. BERNARD

Size: Male, 27½" to 29" high; female, 25½" and up. *Weight:* About 170 pounds. *Standard:* Tall, powerful, strong and muscular in every respect. Massive head, intelligent expression, slightly wrinkled forehead. Ears high-set with strongly developed burr at base. Eyes set to front, slightly pendulous lower lids. Sloping neck, broad back, long tail hanging with slight curve at tip. Short-

Gero Oenz-Bomor, a male nicknamed Hans, is owned and bred by Riverview Kennels, Van Meter, Iowa.

haired variety (most common) has very dense coat, tough but not rough to the touch; long-haired variety has coat of medium length, may be wavy but not curly or shaggy. Colors: red with white or white with red or brindle.

The outstanding characteristic of the St. Bernard, of course, is his size. He is heavy as a man when full grown, but the puppies are balls of fur! Famous in fact and fiction for being a rescuer of travellers lost in the snow, the St. Bernard is also known as Alpine Dog because he gained his fame in the Swiss Alps at the Hospice of St. Bernard. He is never ill-natured, despite the stern look of his visage, and is an ideal dog for the wide open spaces.

Head study of a Saluki owned by Mrs. Esther B. Knapp of Pine Paddocks, Valley City, Ohio. His name, Ch. Mazuri Angel.

Below: 10-week-old Saluki pups from the same kennel. The sire was Ch. Abdul Farouk II; dam, Ch. Rahma Ramullah.

SALUKI

Size: About 23″ to 28″ high. *Weight:* About 60 pounds. *Standard:* Head narrow, close hanging ears, deep narrow chest, long thighs, arched loin. Tall, long and slender. Tail set on low, carried in a graceful curve. Coat fine, smooth and silky. Moderately feathered on back of the legs and tail. Colors: cream, fawn, white, golden, red, or black and tan.

Evidence from the tombs of Egypt's pharaohs tells the story of the founding of civilization, and in this story, the Saluki, or royal dog of Egypt, has his place. Often he was buried with his royal master, and mummies of Salukis have been found in Egypt's tombs. Some of these are now in the British Museum.

Salukis have not changed appreciably in some 6000 years. Once known as gazelle hounds, they were bred by the Arabs to assist in the chase and help supply the people with food. The hound had of necessity to be swift, courageous and untiring. He had as well to satisfy the Arab love for beauty. The same great care was taken in the breeding of dogs as in the breeding of Arabian horses and pedigrees were handed down from generation to generation by word of mouth or song.

SAMOYED

Size: 19″ to 23½″ high. *Weight:* 35 to 65 pounds. *Standard:* A Northern type of dog, squarely built; broad wedge-shaped skull, tapering muzzle, black lips, wide-set slanting eyes, erect furry ears; heavy coat with thick soft under-

Left: Ch. Balalya Doroga Cela, a stylish dog who loves to go to shows and collect blue ribbons. Below: Howling, perhaps, for a nice cool ice floe, is Irish Ch. Rostav of Rozelle imported from Ballygown in the North of Ireland. Both dogs are owned by Mrs. W. R. Ingram, Snowdrift Kennels, Sellers, Alabama.

layer, long outer hairs harsh but shiny, standing out from body. Tail set high, long and thickly furred and feathered, carried over the back. Colors: white and cream.

Named for the ancient Samoyed people of Siberia, the Samoyed long served as hunter, draft dog and herder of reindeer. He still serves as sled dog and pack carrier in polar regions. His heavy coat is adequate protection in the worst kind of weather, and his broad feet find traction on snow and ice alike.

The desirable foxy look is plainly evident in this bright-eyed little Schipperke owned by Fred Blough, Bigster Kennels, Newark, Delaware.

SCHIPPERKE

Size: 12″ to 13″ high. *Weight:* Under 18 pounds. *Standard:* Small, short-bodied, thick-set, compact, powerfully made. Fox-like head fairly wide, narrowing at the eyes, muzzle tapered, not too much stop. Oval eyes, questioning expression, very erect small, triangular ears. Coat abundant, slightly harsh to the touch, heavy undercoat. Hair fairly short except for abundant neck ruff extending down chest and front of forelegs, and equally long culotte on rear. Color: always solid black.

The Schipperke's name is Flemish for "Little Captain." His job was to keep the Belgian canal boats free of rats. When King Leopold II's queen adopted one as a pet in 1885 she set the fashion for this lively, highly inquisitive little dog. Schipperke's outstanding ruff rises even higher whenever his curiosity is excited, and even a closed door or an object moved out of its accustomed place is enough to arouse his interest. He is continually preoccupied with what is going on about him and a sharp bark often accompanies his discovery that something unusual has occurred in the household. He is a hunter of moles and a good dog for hunting rabbits.

SCHNAUZER (Giant, Miniature and Standard)

Size: Giant, 21½" to 25½" high; Standard, 17" to 20" high; Miniature, 11½" to 13½" high. *Weight:* Giant, about 75 pounds; Standard, about 35 pounds; Miniature, about 15 pounds. *Standard:* The three sizes of Schnauzers all have exactly the same characteristics although they are bred and registered as distinct breeds. Sinewy, robust, almost rectangular build, straight strong back, belly well drawn up towards the back. Long head with blunt whiskered muzzle and bristling eyebrows. Small V-shaped ears drop closely to the cheek or stand erect when cropped. Docked tail is carried high. Close, hard, wiry coat. Colors: pepper-and-salt mixtures, pure black or black with tan.

The breeding skill of the Germanic people is well demonstrated in their development of the Schnauzer in three distinct sizes, each breed retaining the splendid physique and keen mental ability that characterize this type of dog. The Standard or medium was the oldest of the three, going back to the 16th century when he was a household favorite as a guard, rat catcher and yard dog. In America and England the Standard is desired as a guard and companion for his devotion and bravery and particularly keen ability to gauge approaching danger. He is also a good water dog and can be easily trained to retrieve. On American sheep ranches he has proven valuable in protecting the flocks against coyotes.

The Giant Schnauzer was developed by Bavarians who liked the Schnauzer but needed a larger dog for driving cattle. They crossed the Standard with a black Great Dane and later with the Bouvier des Flandres, and found that this combination produced an ideal cattle-driving dog and guard. Later in Germany he proved to be an excellent pupil for police work which is his main occupation today. As yet he has not gained widespread popularity in the United States but his high-spirited temperament and reliability are slowly winning friends for him.

By crossing small specimens of Standard with the Affenpinscher, the Miniature Schnauzer came into being as a good household pet. Less aggressive in temperament than his larger brothers, the Miniature is fond of children, hardy, active and intelligent. Though not a fighter he can stand up very well in a fight when necessary, and is a good guard. His size makes him suitable for town and apartment living but he is equally happy in the country where he can run a dozen miles a day, though he seldom wanders. His good health, even temperament and attractive appearance combine to make him increasingly popular.

(See photos on next page.)

Above: The Miniature Schnauzer is the picture of alertness. His owner is Leda B. Martin, Ledahof Kennels, New Brunswick, New Jersey. Left: Ch. Desiree of Tobiah (facing away from the camera) and Ch. Gamala of Tobiah (facing camera) are truly "Giants on Guard." Ch. Desiree was top Giant Schnauzer in 1957 and Ch. Gamala was top Giant in 1958. Both belong to Mr. and Mrs. Thomas W. Bagley, of Germantown, Tennessee.

The dignity, grace and beauty of the Scottish Deerhound are perfectly typified by Ch. Quibba of Enterkine, a superb example. In June, 1959, she was judged Best of Show from among 588 dogs at the Land O'Lakes show in St. Paul. She is owned by Mr. and Mrs. William J. Curran, Blythblue Kennels, Excelsior, Minnesota.

SCOTTISH DEERHOUND

Size: 28″ to 32″ high. *Weight:* 75 to 110 pounds. *Standard:* A large, deep-chested dog with long back arched over the loins. Long, flat head with slight rise but no real stop, pointed muzzle with soft mustache and beard. Small ears set high, folded back except in excitement, long tail carried low and curved. Coat rather long, harsh and wiry except on head, breast and belly, slight fringes on back of forelegs. Colors: dark blue-gray, brindle, yellow, sandy or reddish fawn.

Once called a Rough Greyhound, this breed was so highly prized as a hunter of deer that he almost became extinct during the Middle Ages because of the desire of noblemen to limit his ownership and retain exclusiveness. His size, strength, speed and keen scent account for his pre-eminence as a deer hunter. In the United States, where the hunting of antlered deer with dogs is not allowed, he is a match for any animals that run such as wolves, coyotes and rabbits.

The black and white Scotties have become world-famous, and when Fala lived at the White House he did much to popularize the breed.

SCOTTISH TERRIER

Size: About 10″ high. *Weight:* Male, 19 to 22 pounds; female, 18 to 21 pounds. *Standard:* Principal objective is symmetry and balance. A heavy-boned, small dog with short back, very short legs and wide hindquarters. Head long, muzzle blunt with not too much taper toward the nose. Jaws level and square. Eyes piercingly bright, set wide apart. Ears small, pricked, set well up on skull, pointed but not cut. Coat rather short, dense undercoat with outercoat intensely hard and wiry. Seven-inch tail carried up in a moderate curve. Colors: steel or iron gray, brindled or grizzled, black, sandy or wheat.

The "Scottie" gives the impression of immense power in small size. One of the most ancient breeds, the Scottish Terrier from the Highlands is said by some to be the original Terrier. The Scottie has bred in purity for many years with the essentials of the standard retained. The standards in Scotland and England differ only slightly from the American standards.

Originally a hunter of all kinds of vermin, the Scottie makes an ideal house pet requiring only small quarters.

SEALYHAM TERRIER

Size: About 10½" high. *Weight:* 20 to 21 pounds. *Standard:* Very low on the legs, moderately short in back, a tough little fellow with big bones. Skull slightly domed with shallow indentation running between brows. Jaws level, powerful and square. Eyes very dark and deeply set. Ears folded level with top of head with forward edge close to cheek. Tail docked and carried straight up. Coat weather-resisting with soft dense undercoat and hard wiry topcoat. Colors: all white or with lemon, tan or badger markings on head and ears.

Between 1850 and 1891, this terrier was developed from obscure ancestry in Sealyham, Wales. His ancestors were noted for their prowess in quarrying badger, otter and fox. The Sealyham is extremely game and has an endurance that is great for a dog so small. The breed first appeared at a show in Wales in 1903, in England in 1910, and then in America in 1911.

The Sealyham's ability to dig and battle underground is little used in city living but the small dog is popular in small quarters.

The handsome Sealyham belongs to Mrs. J. Barnes, Westfield, New Jersey.

SHETLAND SHEEPDOG

Size: 13″ to 16″ high. *Weight:* About 16 pounds. *Standard:* Miniature but otherwise identical to the Collie; graceful, fairly long, rounded body. Heavy coat with long mane and frill, feathered legs and tail. Head tapering towards slanting eyes; slender, clean-cut muzzle; small, semi-erect ears. Tail long, carried low with slight upward swirl. Colors: sable, tricolor or blue merle with white markings.

This dog comes from a land where everything, of necessity, is miniature. Like the ponies for which the rocky, barren Shetland Isles are also famous, the Shetland Sheepdog is a small version of a larger animal. Bred to mind sheep, he makes a delightful companion, frisky and affectionate and not too large to be a housedog. He is still considered indispensable on many Western American ranches where he works as a herder with proficiency, loyalty and stamina. "Shelties," as they are familiarly known, are outstanding winners in obedience work, often garnering as much as 50 per cent of the A.K.C. awards at obedience trials.

Here you can see the relative size of Sheltie and Collie, as well as their great similarity. In the foreground is Vivid Technique of Hobby Ho, owned by Mrs. Jean Charron, Melodylane Sheltie Kennels, Chesterton, New York. Standing behind her is To Kalon Bold Ruler II, a Rough Collie owned by Mr. and Mrs. Frederick Smith of Seaford, New York.

Lead dog in the Monadnock Kennels' prize-winning team of Siberian Huskies is Ch. Monadnock Pando. Pando himself holds an all-time record for the breed for show wins, and has sired many successful young Siberians of the show ring. Mr. and Mrs. Nicholas Demidoff are the owners of Monadnock Kennels in Fitzwilliam, New Hampshire.

SIBERIAN HUSKY

Size: 20" to 23½" high. *Weight:* 35 to 50 pounds. *Standard:* Compact, powerful, muscular, alert, typically northern. Finely chiseled skull and muzzle, furred pointed ears held erect, slightly slanting eyes. Coat very soft, dense, downy undercoat and smooth, silky outer coat; clean-cut appearance. Heavily furred tail arched over back. Colors: all colors including white, often with varied and striking markings including cap-like mask and spectacles.

An extremely versatile dog, the Siberian Husky has been purebred for centuries and treasured as sled dog, work dog and companion for their children by the Chuchis of Siberia. It is not surprising, therefore, that he adapts well to being a pet with his friendly companionship and love of children, clean habits and odorlessness and modest eating demands. He adjusts well to warmer climates and is not a noisy neighbor in the city.

111

SILKY TERRIER (Australian)

Size: About 10″ high. *Weight:* 6 to 12 pounds. *Standard:* (Not yet recognized by A.K.C.) Compact body, long in proportion to its height. V-shaped ears erect and free from long hair, topknot silver-blue. Fine silky coat, about 6″ long. Docked tail carried erect. Color: blue and tan.

Alert and very active, the Australian Silky Terrier's compact little body makes him a hardy companion for the country as well as the city. Although he is not yet recognized by the A.K.C., the popularity of the Silky Terrier is fast on the rise.

Delalor Banjo Bluespec of Iradell Kennels, owned by Mrs. N. Clarkson Earl, Jr., of Ridgefield, Connecticut.

SKYE TERRIER

Size: About 10" high at shoulder and 37½" in length, with an ideal ratio of two to one in body length to shoulder height. *Weight:* About 28 to 33 pounds. *Standard:* Long, low body looks slender because of pear-shaped ribs. Short straight legs with feet pointing forward. Long tapered head on long graceful neck; powerful jaws; dark eyes rather closely set; ears either prick or drop. Double coat—soft woolly undercoat and hard, straight and flat outercoat which veils head and hangs heavily from ears, underbody and legs. Well-feathered tail, not carried above the level of the back, usually hangs down. Muzzle, ears and tail tip usually dark but head and legs same shade as body. Colors: any color, including black, dark or light blue, gray, fawn or cream.

The Skye Terrier of nearly four centuries ago looked almost exactly like his present-day counterpart, unlike most terriers who developed to their present form within the last century. According to an old historic volume called *Englishe Dogges,* he was "brought out of the barbarous borders" of the Skye mountains in Scotland where his flowing coat protected him admirably from the attacks of vicious wild animals as well as from the extremes of weather and rough terrain. He became a fashionable court dog and the fact that he remains practically unchanged after four centuries proves the strong attachment of his followers. Reserved with strangers, he is a deeply devoted one-family dog. He is alert, fearless, good-tempered and capable of showing much stamina, strength and agility in overtaking game. He is adaptable to town life as well as to country and makes an excellent watchdog.

113

Obediently quiet but raring to go is Ch. Glamour Girl, one of the 12 champions sired by Ch. X-Pert Brindle Biff. Glamour Girl is owned by Mr. and Mrs. Clifford A. Ormsby, X-Pert Staf-Terrier Kennels, Hornell, New York.

STAFFORDSHIRE TERRIER

Size: 17" to 19" high. *Weight:* 30 to 50 pounds. *Standard:* Broad-chested and short-backed with forelegs set wide and well-muscled hind legs. Head is broad with medium-long muzzle, semi-erect ears and wide-set eyes. Short, stiff coat; long, tapering, low-set tail. Colors: any color or combination of colors, brindled, parti-colored or patched.

Bred originally for pit fighting, the Staffordshire Terrier is known also as the Pit Bull Terrier. He has also been known in America as the Yankee Terrier, though he comes from Staffordshire, England, as the name implies. The fierce, stern face of the Staffordshire hides one of the sweetest dispositions of any breed of dog. He is an ideal dog for home and show.

WEIMARANER

Size: Male, 25″ to 27″ high; female, 23″ to 25″ high. *Weight:* 55 to 85 pounds, females proportionately lighter. *Standard:* A medium-sized gray dog with light eyes, he presents a picture of great driving power, stamina and alertness, and indicates his ability to work hard in the field. Head moderately long and aristocratic. Flews moderately deep enclosing powerful jaw. Lips and gums pinkish flesh shades. Ears long and lobular. Expression kind, keen and intelligent. Skin tightly drawn. Coat short, smooth and sleek. Walk rather awkward, trot effortless. Colors: shades of mouse-gray to silver-gray.

An all-around sporting dog of German origin, the Weimaraner dates back only to the early 19th century but the Bloodhound is believed to be one of his ancestors. He is cousin to the German Shorthaired Pointer and in fact, was known previously as the Weimar Pointer. Since then, height and weight have both been increased.

The Weimaraner is distinctive for his coat color and light-color eyes. Formerly a big-game dog, the breed is now highly prized by amateur sportsmen who breed for sport rather than for profit. America did not know the Weimaraner until about 1929. In both Germany and America the dog has been used more as a personal hunting companion than as a field trial competitor. The Weimaraner is accustomed to being a member of the family, accepts the responsibility it entails and is not happy when relegated to the kennel.

The Weimaraner can learn to stand motionless on signal. This beautiful dog is owned by Stanley A. Bogan of Butler, New Jersey.

A pair of Corgis enjoy a romp with their master.

WELSH CORGI (Pembroke and Cardigan)

Size: 10″ to 12″ high. *Weight:* Pembroke male, 20 to 24 pounds; female, 18 to 22 pounds. Cardigan male, 18 to 25 pounds; female, 15 to 22 pounds. *Standard:* Cardigan—Low-slung, Dachshund-like, long, strong little dog. Deep chest, small waist, short legs, long tail. Pembroke legs are longer, tail naturally short or docked. Both have foxy head. Cardigan has short, thick and hard coat; Pembroke coat of medium length and dense, not wiry. Colors of both: red, black and tan, and blue merle. Cardigan also can be brindled and black and white. Pembroke can also be fawn and brindled without white marking.

Both are ancient breeds. The Corgi has come to be a show specimen only in very recent times. Some authorities refuse to link the two types of Corgis under the heading of a single breed. The Pembroke seems similar in some ways to the Schipperke while the Cardigan, 3000 years old, seems to be of the same family as the Dachshund. Noticeable differences occur in the ears and tail— Cardigan's ears being round, and the Pembroke's pointed at the tip and standing erect. In disposition the Pembroke is more restless and more easily excited. Some of the resemblances occur because the two were crossed before the middle of the 19th century and they seem to be growing closer together in selective breeding. More recently the practice has been stopped and breeders today are determined to keep the Pembroke distinct from the Cardigan. A Pembroke is a very agreeable small house dog as he has an affectionate nature and does not force his attentions on anyone unwilling to accept them.

WELSH SPRINGER SPANIEL

Size: About 17″ high. *Weight:* About 40 pounds. *Standard:* Moderate length head with straight fairly square muzzle (not chubby); flesh-colored or dark nostrils; hazel or dark eyes; ears hang moderately low, close to the cheeks, covered with setter-like feathering. Strong, muscular body, medium length straight legs with round thickly padded feet. Thick coat, silky texture, straight or flat, never wiry nor wavy, soft undercoat. Colors: dark rich red and white.

Old writings and pictures dating back as far as the 16th century reveal that hunters used a spaniel closely resembling the Welsh Springer. He is an excellent retriever from the water, with remarkable stamina, and will stay with a cripple to the point of drowning. He is equally good hunting any kind of game but must be well trained: he has such a keen nose that he tends to be a

Dein Glynis of Randhaven, first female Welsh Springer Spaniel Champion in the U. S. A., is owned and bred by H. R. and E. B. Randolph of Randhaven Kennels, in Medford Station, Long Island, N. Y.

lone hunter otherwise. The Springer is principally found in Wales where he is a close member of the family circle because of his lovable, stable temperament. He is a good guard, usually gentle with children and other animals, and easy to keep. His thick coat enables him to withstand extremes of heat and cold as well as water and injury from thorns. He can live in town and be happy but is ideal for the country as a gun dog.

Family pet Ch. Carlano Canakin loves cats, according to owner Carl F. Neumann of Wheaton, Illinois, and the neighbor's cats swarm into this Welsh Terrier's backyard to play with her.

WELSH TERRIER

Size: 14″ to 15″ high. *Weight:* About 20 pounds. *Standard:* Short back, moderately wide chest, muscular thighs, strong legs. Head wider than most terriers, deep muzzle, powerful jaws. Small V-shaped ears drop forward close to cheeks. Docked tail stands straight up. Thick coat wiry and hard. Colors: black and tan, or black grizzle and tan.

After 100 years or more, the Welsh Terrier of today has changed very little from the Black-and-Tan Wire-Haired Terrier he used to be known as. In his native home of Wales, he was used extensively for hunting the otter, fox, and badger, and to this day he possesses the gameness of a sporting dog. Not the least bit quarrelsome, he is well mannered and easy to handle.

WEST HIGHLAND WHITE TERRIER

Size: 10″ to 11″ high. *Weight:* 13-19 pounds. *Standard:* Short, compact body on straight legs. Wide, well-developed hindquarters. Narrow skull is as long as the muzzle. Wide-set bright eyes and small, pointed erect ears. Hard coat 2″ in length. Tail about 5″ to 6″ long, carried gaily. Color: white.

"Westies," like most terriers, are active and intelligent. The alert, foxy look which is so characteristic of this breed expresses perfectly the personality of the playful dog—a friendly, companionable pet and a fine watchdog. "A big dog in a small package," the West Highland White Terrier, as his name implies, must always be white. However, his coat is easy to keep clean as the straight, rough hairs shed soil easily, and a good brushing leaves the coat white and sparkling.

This West Highland White Terrier knows what's good for him. The stiff brush not only restores the whiteness to his coat; it makes him feel like a million, too. Gray-Kings Rob Spark Durham is owned by Martha Gray King Miller, Kennel and Cattery, Binghamton, N.Y.

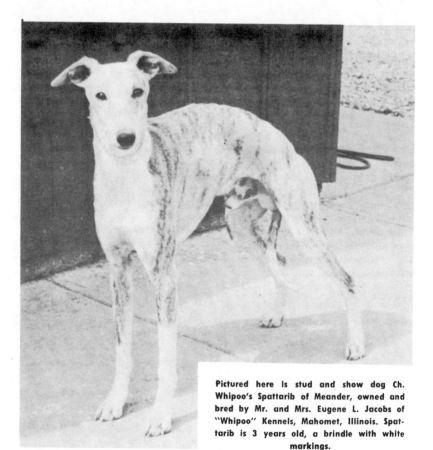

Pictured here is stud and show dog Ch. Whipoo's Spattarib of Meander, owned and bred by Mr. and Mrs. Eugene L. Jacobs of "Whipoo" Kennels, Mahomet, Illinois. Spattarib is 3 years old, a brindle with white markings.

WHIPPET

Size: 18″ to 22″ high. *Weight:* 10 to 28 pounds. *Standard:* Long and lean head fairly wide between the ears, powerful muzzle; large, intelligent eyes with keen, alert expression, dark as coat color; well-arched and muscular neck widening gradually to shoulders; long, powerful hindquarters with tapering long tail reaching to hipbone when drawn through between the hind legs; low, free moving and smooth gait. Coat close, smooth and firm in texture. Colors: various.

The Whippet is an English Greyhound in miniature, a top-flight sporting dog as well as an affectionate and intelligent pet. A relatively new breed of only 75 to 100 years, it's said that the Whippet evolved when the sporting gentry tired of barbaric pastimes such as bull- and bear-baiting and dog-fighting and bred the Whippet for the "milder" entertainment of watching him course rabbits in an enclosure. Later the Whippet was used primarily for straight racing. His speed comes close to 35 miles per hour and he runs with extreme grace, beauty and smoothness of action. The Whippet is exceptionally keen when racing or on game, quiet, dignified and beautiful in the living room.

YORKSHIRE TERRIER

Size: 8" to 9" high. *Weight:* 4 to 8 pounds. *Standard:* General appearance of long-haired toy terrier, coat hanging neatly down each side from a parting extending from the nose to the end of the tail. Head rather small and flat. Body short; compact and level back. Tail docked. Eyes dark and sparkling. Ears erect or semi-erect. Color: blue and tan, hair darker at roots than in middle, shading to still lighter tan at tips.

Named for the county of Yorkshire in England, the Yorkshire was developed as recently as 1861. Probably a development from the Skye Terrier

Giving a Yorkshire his beauty treatment is part of his care. The dog pictured is from Grandeur Kennels of Sunny Shay in Hicksville, Long Island, N. Y.

which was definitely Scotch, the Yorkshire Terrier was first called the Scotch Terrier. The Yorkshire in time became the fashionable pet of ladies of the aristocracy and of wealthy families in the late Victorian era. The breed has been reduced in size until it can now be called a toy. There were undoubtedly crosses with the Maltese and the Dandie Dinmont Terrier. The Yorkshire was introduced to America by 1880.

The Yorkshire's topknot and coloring are distinctive. Although at various times a greatly pampered toy, the Yorkshire is a spirited dog. His extreme length of coat presents a problem for owners who must keep their dogs in the house. Even his feet must be booted or stockinged so that in scratching he will not ruin his gloriously fine coat.

INDEX